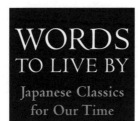

WORDS
TO LIVE BY
Japanese Classics
for Our Time

JAPAN LIBRARY

WORDS
TO LIVE BY
Japanese Classics
for Our Time

Nakano Kōji

TRANSLATED BY
Juliet Winters Carpenter

Japan Publishing Industry Foundation for Culture

TRANSLATION NOTE

The Hepburn system of Romanization is used for Japanese terms, including the names of persons and places. Except in familiar place names, long vowels are indicated by macrons. Japanese names are given in Japanese order, family name first, except for those with established identities under Western-style names. Ages of premodern people follow traditional Japanese reckoning, which counts a person as one year old at birth. Transliterations are provided for *waka* and haiku but not for *kanshi*.

Words to Live by: Japanese Classics for Our Time
Nakano Kōji. Translated by Juliet Winters Carpenter

Published by Japan Publishing Industry Foundation for Culture (JPIC)
3-12-3 Kanda-Jinbocho, Chiyoda-ku, Tokyo 101-0051, Japan

First English edition: March 2018

© Kanagawa Bungaku Shinkokai 2017
English translation © 2017 by Japan Publishing Industry Foundation for Culture

Originally published in Japanese under the title *Ima o ikiru chie*, by Iwanami Shoten in 2002. The English edition is a revised and abridged edition of the original.

English publishing rights arranged with Iwanami Shoten, Publishers, Tokyo.

Jacket and cover design by Miki Kazuhiko, Ampersand Works

As this book is published primarily to be donated to overseas universities, research institutions, public libraries and other organizations, commercial publication rights are available. For all enquiries regarding those rights, please contact the publisher of the English edition at the following address: japanlibrary@jpic.or.jp

Printed in Japan
ISBN 978-4-86658-024-1
http://www.jpic.or.jp/japanlibrary/

C O N T E N T S

P R E F A C E

On April 7, 1991, NHK direct satellite broadcasting launched a program called Weekly Book Review on which I was a regular guest. Over the next ten years, up to the time of my retirement last spring, I made some fifty appearances. The staff never varied, and over the years we formed lasting friendships. When I retired from the show, one of the producers, Nomizu Kiyoshi, who had read my books and knew that I wrote frequently about classical writers of Japan and their works, then invited me to appear on an educational NHK radio program to discuss the classics. I had no objection to talking on the radio, but I warned him that much of what I said would overlap with my writing. Devising all-new talks would have been too exhausting a proposition for me to consider. Nomizu said basing my talks on what I had already written would be fine.

In all there were twenty-six weekly broadcasts of thirty minutes each, running from April through September of this year. I undertook the project with the notion that all I needed to do was read aloud some of my previous writings, but after the first two recording sessions I realized my mistake. Preparing five or six decent segments on the same writer with new information each time meant I had to rethink all my material and devise new ways of organizing and presenting it.

So began the demanding task of working up a dozen or more talks to be broadcast twice a day. I was comforted to learn that despite the difficulty of the content, response was positive, and many listeners tuned in. Radio, I discovered, attracts a far more enthusiastic audience than television. NHK released the content of my talks ahead of time in textbook form, and again I was surprised at the positive reception, although due to editorial changes the textbook was not exactly the same as the talks I recorded.

Then Yamaguchi Akio of Iwanami Shoten listened to tapes of the show and told me, to my great pleasure, that he was interested in publishing my talks in book form. The present book, therefore, unlike the NHK textbook, is based directly on my radio talks. I believe that the rhythm of my delivery will come through to readers.

Six writers are introduced here: Ryōkan, Yoshida Kenkō, Kamo no Chō-mei, Dōgen, Saigyō, and Yosa Buson. My perspective remained constant while reading and contemplating each of the masters, finding related elements throughout. If this book encourages others to take an interest in the classics of Japan and delve into them for themselves, nothing would make me happier.

Nakano Kōji
December 2001

Ryōkan

1758–1831

Yasuda Yukihiko, *Portrait of Master Ryōkan*
(detail), Ryōkan Memorial Museum

A Zen monk, poet and calligrapher. He was born in the town of Izumozaki in Echigo Province (present-day Niigata Prefecture). His name in childhood was Eizō, later Fumitaka; his sobriquet was Magari. At age 18 he entered Kōshōji temple and was ordained a monk. At age 22 he became the student of Zen master Tainin Kokusen and accompanied him to Entsūji temple in present-day Okayama Prefecture, where eleven years later he received a certificate of enlightenment. The following year, after Kokusen's passing, Ryōkan left to spend five years wandering about the country. Then he returned to Echigo but not to his parents' home, instead living on or near Mt. Kugami. From around age 47 he lived in a hermitage called Gogō-an. At age 60 he moved to a grass hut in Otogo Shrine and at 69 to a detached room on the grounds of the Kimura residence. He died at the age of 74. He is famous for his Chinese poetry, *waka*, and calligraphy. Thanks also in part to his simple and pure life, he is highly regarded today.

1

A Mysterious Charm

Ryōkan the Man

In these talks I am going to introduce some of my favorite Japanese writers from ages past. I won't get into formal discussions of their works, but select favorite passages and consider them in the light of today. I will discuss only writers whose works I turn to often with pleasure.

We'll start with the Zen monk Ryōkan, an intriguing character whose poetry I love. He wrote mostly *waka*, short poems in phrases of 5-7-5-7-7 syllabic units, as well as a few other nonstandard forms, and *kanshi*, verses of even-numbered lines written in Chinese. His poems give a remarkably clear picture of his character and create a sense of immediacy.

muragimono	Joy
kokoro tanoshi mo	fills my heart
haru no hi ni	on a spring day
tori no muragari	seeing a flock of
asobu o mireba	birds at play.

This declaration of the happiness the poet feels in spring watching a playful flock of birds is simple and straightforward, yet it gracefully conveys his delight in the coming of spring. Ryōkan's poems generally are easy to understand, direct, gentle, and warm; they appeal straight to the heart. This *waka* has all those qualities in spades. For Ryōkan, winter meant the harsh northern climate of Echigo (today's Niigata Prefecture), facing the Japan Sea. He lived in a grass hut, a rough shelter without adequate heat or protection from icy blasts. After the rigors of winter he would have been overjoyed at the coming of spring; the first half of the poem must have come to him easily. Then he happened to see a flock of playful birds, also reveling in the spring day, and felt a bond with them. It's as if the poem wrote itself. It is unpretentious and endearing, and reading it one cannot help feeling close to Ryōkan as he rejoices in spring.

Ryōkan's *kanshi*, while cavalier with the rules of Chinese meter, have a similar directness and candor. Reading them, one enters into his feelings and is caught up pleasurably in them. All his poems express his humanity and his appealing personality. Yet somehow when I try to picture Ryōkan as he actually was, I am unsure. He recedes again, his figure now blurred and hazy. For a long time I found this puzzling.

Ryōkan is immensely popular in Japan. He became well known during the Meiji period, and over the ensuing 150 years or so his fame has only grown. All across Japan there are study societies in honor of him and his works, and books and academic studies appear regularly. A visitor to Niigata Prefecture will come across various Ryōkan-related monuments as well as several museums dedicated to him.

What makes Ryōkan so popular? After mulling it over, I came up with an answer that may be a bit surprising. I think it comes down to the vast difference between his way of life and ours. Our worlds are poles apart. He lived in thatched huts, first a tiny one on Mt. Kugami called "Gogō-an," and he owned next to nothing. (*Gogō* means the amount of rice needed for daily sustenance.) I have visited Gogō-an several times, and I can attest that it is a small, humble place. When he lived there, probably all it had was a sunken hearth with a small pot and a few random dishes he'd picked up. The wooden floor would have been covered with a straw mat on which he spread wafer-thin bedding, hardly enough to stave off the cold. His wardrobe consisted of one black monk's robe. On his writing-table were an inkstone and brush, nothing fancy. He owned next to nothing, yet his poetry and calligraphy speak volumes.

Fond as I am of Ryōkan, my lifestyle is vastly different from his. I turn a tap to get hot water. I have a washing machine, a refrigerator, and a rice cooker, as well as heating and air conditioning; I am blessed with every sort of convenience and creature comfort. If I feel unwell, I have recourse to medicine, hospitals, and medical insurance. Ryōkan's health wasn't very good; he frequently caught cold or suffered from diarrhea. What sort of medicine or treatment, if any, was available to him? Some of his poems indicate that when he was sick all he could do was crawl into bed.

Ryōkan and I share a love of reading, but whereas I can buy all the books I want, he had to borrow his. When he heard that someone had bought a copy of the *Collection of Ten Thousand Leaves*—the great mid-eighth-century poetry anthology, just then becoming the focus of sustained study—he begged permission to borrow it and then proceeded to teach himself to read the fiendishly difficult writing system it uses. He also borrowed Dōgen's *Treasury of the True Dharma Eye*, another extraordinarily difficult book. Many letters survive in which he asks to borrow books.

Ryōkan's calligraphy is celebrated. People were always begging him to write something for them, which he would do using a worn brush and a humble inkstone. I, on the other hand, am particular about the writing implements I use, buying only antique inkstones and fine-quality inks and brushes.

The difference between Ryōkan's way of life and ours is truly night and day. We are affluent, but he was penniless and unattached. Although he was a Zen monk, for most of his life he was unaffiliated with any temple or monastery and had no protection of any kind, living alone in a kind of wind-swept existence. We revere him because, I would suggest, his approach to life gives us a sense that he had an inner treasure we lack.

By and large, the twentieth century was an age of ideology and war, but at the same time, people who had strong faith in human progress invented everything from automobiles and television to computers and mobile phones. Life became more and more convenient, though whether people became any happier is doubtful. Certainly during Japan's postwar period of high economic growth it *felt* as if we were getting happier by the day, as all sorts of new products came on the market and every day brought fresh progress of some kind. But eventually that all came to an end. The economic bubble burst, and the final decade of the twentieth century was a time of deep skepticism concerning the connection between material progress and happiness. It became clear that the mere proliferation of things could not make us happy. Instead, we became so focused on our possessions that we were bound to them, no longer free. This background helps explain why Ryōkan, a man who was effortlessly happy while owning nothing, has become the object of widespread interest and veneration.

Calm and Leisurely Living

Ryōkan was patient and easygoing by nature, but he disliked talk that was loquacious, glib, impertinent, or boastful, and he called offenders to task in a work entitled *Words of Warning*. Reading it made clear to me that not only I but all modern people—certainly television celebrities—talk too fast and too much. Our lives are hectic, our schedules crammed full and planned to the minute, but Ryōkan liked calm and leisurely living. The stark contrast between him and us in terms of lifestyle, personality, temperament, and interests points to the nature of true happiness.

I suggested earlier that behind Ryōkan's delight in the coming of spring lay his recent bitter experience of winter. The human tendency is to value something more when we have been deprived of it, less when we enjoy it easily. Little things we mostly take for granted loomed large to Ryōkan precisely because he lived in a state of constant deprivation or *mu*, nothingness.

uzumibi ni	Lying down tonight
ashi sashikubete	with my feet stretched out
fuseredomo	by the banked fire—
koyoi no samusa	the freezing cold goes
hara ni tōrinu	straight to my belly.

"Banked fire" refers to the lingering warmth in the ashes in the hearth at the end of the day. The poet Saitō Mokichi (1882–1953) effusively praised the last line, which has the unmistakable ring of reality. This is how Ryōkan lived—sleeping on a thin mat spread on a wooden floor, cold air seeping through the cracks. His wooden walls were not mud-plastered, and with no insulation, the wind and cold could sweep right in. Such dire experiences intensified his keen enjoyment of spring. His poetry and calligraphy are the product of a life lived in circumstances so straitened that we would find them unbearable. The mystery of Ryōkan, and of human life in general, lies in the fact that a bare-bones lifestyle can give rise to sublime art.

Examine any poem by Ryōkan, and it will clearly be the fruit of his penniless, wind-swept existence. What makes the poetry of this man whose lifestyle was a world away from ours so affecting, so poignant and so endearing? His life experiences and mine are so different that it would seem as if nothing could possibly connect us, yet I find his works exert a strangely powerful influence on me.

His Mere Presence

My interest in Ryōkan has taken me to all sorts of historical sites connected with him. When he first went to live in his mountain hut as a mendicant monk, he must have been the object of suspicion, contempt, and disdain, but gradually, as his amiable personality and nobility of spirit became known along with his gifts as a calligrapher and man of culture, even powerful village headmen came to hold him in high esteem. Ryōkan never presumed upon these men's goodwill, which I believe he earned because they saw in his eccentricity an enviable freedom and richness of spirit. Their former homes still stand near sites commemorating Ryōkan's life and works. The Abe, Kera, Kimura, and other families that once wielded vast power and wealth accumulated an assortment of items related to Ryōkan.

The Kera residence contains a biography by Kera Yoshishige (1810–1859), *Curious Accounts of the Zen Monk Ryōkan,* in which Ryōkan's personality shines through. Here is an excerpt:

The master stayed two nights in our house. Everyone, older and younger alike, is drawn to him. The house was filled with a spirit of harmony, and even after he had gone, for several days our hearts were warm. An evening of talking with him makes you feel purified from within. Yet he never expounds on scripture, Buddhist or otherwise, or urges you to do good. He goes to the kitchen and builds a fire or sits in the main room, quietly meditating. He doesn't talk about poetry and literature or even morals. Yet his bearing is calm and relaxed, with an indescribable grace. His mere presence has power to restore people to morality.[1]

---

1 Matsumoto Ichiju, *Ryōkan* (Tokyo: Haruki Bunko, 2000).

I love this firsthand account of Ryōkan as someone who had a subtly transformative impact on people.

The Kera house has been torn down, but in its day it was a vast residence. The floor plan, which I have seen, indicates that the house was by modern standards impossibly big—so much so that Ryōkan's two-night stay could have gone almost unnoticed. And yet his presence even for that short time put everyone in a good mood, soothing and calming them. He didn't preach or do much of anything, really. He simply lit a kitchen fire or sat in meditation, "his mere presence" acting like a balm. He was friendly, yet maintained an innate dignity. This description corresponds closely to Ryōkan's image today in Japan, an image shaped by his poetry.

And yet, as I said earlier, every time I try to form an overall picture of the man, my thoughts get in a muddle. Finally I came to see that he lived by a principle fundamentally different from ours: Where we follow the principle of *yūi*, active existence, he followed the principle of *mui*, inaction. Where we seek to possess things, he owned nothing. Where we seek to gain, he sought to cast aside. Where we strive to attain a certain condition, he left all to fate. Where we belong to a company or some other organization, he was completely on his own, unaffiliated with any temple or town. His life is the converse of ours; he turns everything on its head. He was a hermit of transcendent appeal. Therein lies the mystery of Ryōkan.

2

Taking Religious Vows

An Introverted Youth

The story of the monk Ryōkan begins with his decision to take religious vows, but long before that he was Yamamoto Eizō, the son of Tachibanaya Yamamoto in the town of Izumozaki, Echigo. In the natural order of things he would have succeeded to his father's position as village headman and gone on to burnish the luster of the family name. At first he was being groomed to do so, but then he began attending a school run by Ōmori Shiyō, a scholar of Chinese learning, and found scholarship more to his taste.

Local schoolteacher Nishigōri Kyūgo gives this account of what Ryōkan was like at the time:

> His character was foolish, honest, and taciturn. He was easygoing and had few wants. The company of others didn't interest him; instead he was always absorbed in a book. He was incapable of tidying his appearance to meet someone. People said the village headman's son was as useless as "a lantern in the daytime." His parents were worried.[2]

---

2   Nishigōri Kyūgo, *Hokuetsu ijin shamon Ryōkan zenden* (Tokyo: Shozansha, 1980).

All sorts of stories survive about Ryōkan, adding up to more or less the same picture: a youth who was uncommunicative, vacant-minded, slow, had few wants, and was indifferent to social interaction. He loved to read, which suggests that he was an introverted young man who spent more time alone indoors reading and cogitating than he did playing outdoors with his friends—the sort of person who is shy and sensitive, less taken up with outer events than with the stirrings of his own heart.

The Kera biography also includes this comment: "He was even-tempered, not given to joy or anger, never heard to rattle on. Whether eating, drinking, getting up or lying down, his actions were so slow and labored that at first he seemed simple-minded." This is a description of Ryōkan in old age, but he sounds the same as in his youth, his personality and behavior unchanged. Clearly he was never cut out to be village headman, a job requiring knowledge of the world and considerable social skills. A village headman had to be closely involved with the world, ideally an extrovert who would enjoy dealing with people and jockeying for power. But to Ryōkan, such things were annoying or unbearable. Although he was being trained as his father's successor, I suspect he had no stomach for the job. Right about then someone else in his home village had grown influential and was engaged in an ugly power struggle with his father, which would only have put him off public life all the more.

Devoted to Zen Training

Various theories have been put forward concerning Ryōkan's decision to undertake Zen discipline. My own opinion is that he grew tired of dealing with a world swirling with malevolent desires and trouble and decided his only choice was to flee. He seems to have decided to become a monk in 1775, at age eighteen. His motivation wasn't the discovery of impermanence or the desire to enter on the path of Buddhism. I think he just wanted to turn his back on the messiness of life.

When Ryōkan was twenty-two, a Zen master named Kokusen came to town, and Ryōkan ended up going with him to the Sōtō Zen monastery Entsūji in Tamashima, Bichū (today's Kurashiki, Okayama Prefecture). He stayed there for thirteen years, until Kokusen's death in 1791.

Kokusen was a strict follower of the teachings of Dōgen, the founder of the Sōtō school of Zen, and Ryōkan's training under him was rigorous. They would get up around three in the morning for *zazen*, seated meditation. Then all day long until late at night they would alternate this with *samu*, physical work done as a spiritual practice. This went on day after day. Ryōkan wrote a number of poems reflecting back on those days, including this Chinese poem entitled "Entsūji":

Since I came to Entsūji
How many winters and springs have passed?
When my kimono becomes grimy I wash it myself;
When there is no more food I go out begging.
Before the temple gate, a thousand houses—
Not a single person there is known to me.
I read the lives of eminent monks of old.
Be content with honest poverty, they say.

In this way, Ryōkan devoted himself conscientiously to his training. However slow-witted he may have seemed back home, he took to monastic life with a will. Buddhism under the protection of the shogunate had grown lax and corrupt. So-called "funerary Buddhism," with its focus on lucrative funeral rites, dates from this time. A majority of Ryōkan's peers, however many there may have been, no doubt had worldly goals in entering the monastery and looked forward to receiving a certification of enlightenment so they could move on to become head of a temple somewhere and enjoy an easy life. Ryōkan, however, was there for purely spiritual reasons and devoted himself wholeheartedly to monastic life. Above all, he internalized the principle of forsaking things.

Dōgen's Teachings

Perhaps nowhere in Japan were the teachings of Dōgen as faithfully observed as at Entsūji. Kokusen saw to it that his disciples were well versed in Dōgen's masterwork, *Treasury of the True Dharma Eye*. Ryōkan committed many passages to heart and remembered them for the rest of his life. Here is one such passage, from the chapter "Ceaseless Practice":

> If you would ceaselessly practice the Great Way of the Buddhists and patriarchs now, do not go on about greater hermits and lesser hermits or who is quick-witted and who is a dunce. Simply discard fame and profit, and do not let yourself be tied in bonds.... If you are attached to home, detach yourself from home; if you have bonds of affection, detach yourself from bonds of affection; if you have a good name, detach yourself from your good name; if you own fields and gardens, get rid of them; if you have family, detach yourself from family.

Turn aside from all things and devote yourself wholly to the path of Buddhism: this is Dōgen's advice. Ryōkan took these words to heart and obeyed them almost to a fault.

Dōgen wrote often that monks in training should be poor, and here too Ryōkan took him at his word. A compilation of talks by Dōgen called *Treasury of the True Dharma Eye: Record of Things Heard* contains the following passage:

One day an acolyte came to me and asked the proper attitude for one learning the Way. I told him that to begin with, a monk should definitely be poor. If he has great property, he is bound to lose incentive to do spiritual training. A monk in training should possess three robes and a bowl, and that's all. He shouldn't seek comfort or crave clothes and food. If he devotes himself wholeheartedly to study of the Way, he will reap all manner of benefits.

Dōgen repeats this advice over and over, and Ryōkan took it seriously. Here is my interpretation of what it means. Human desires know no limits, so without reins people quickly became enslaved to lust for everything from money and possessions to power and supremacy, sex and food, and the exercise of control over others. Even if the human heart was originally pure, as Buddhism teaches, amid the strife of this world our desires grow until before we know it we are vessels of lust. Trapped by our desires, we lose our innate freedom of spirit. This is why Dōgen urges people to recapture their original purity of heart by abandoning desire, fleeing power relations as well as bonds of love and obligation, and practicing the Way. That philosophy was the making of Ryōkan.

In his book *Ryōkan*, the philosopher and critic Karaki Junzō makes this observation:

Why do people turn their backs on fame, fortune and worldly ties, and leave home to seek the Way? Because their true self is buried or restrained by fame, fortune, and worldly ties. Undertaking the path of Buddhism, of Zen, means "learning the self," that is, discovering one's true self—what is also called "investigation of the self." That is the starting point and the ending point of Buddhism. Therein lies the pilgrimage of studying the Dharma under a master as well as practicing the Way, shedding body and mind, and returning to the self. After forty years of practice, realization comes: the self is merely the self. "In heaven and on earth, I alone am holy"[3] comes to the same thing, as does the realization that one is always alone, in life and in death. The self exists of itself. To be self-possessed and free is to be genuine.[4]

This passage is, I think, an eloquent explanation of the injunction to cast off fame, riches, and all ties.

What Karaki calls "investigation of the self" is invoked toward the beginning of Treasury of the True Dharma Eye in these words: "To learn the way of Buddhism is to learn the self. To learn the self is to forget the self. To forget the self is to become one with universal truth. To become one with universal truth is to shed ideas of 'my body and mind' and 'others' bodies and minds.'" In other words, to learn Buddhism is not to learn something outside oneself but to learn—to investigate—oneself. To take up the study of oneself means to forget oneself. Consciousness of the self disappears, and then the very self disappears. When nothing is left, the Dharma enters—Dharma, or universal truth, being a Sanskrit word that means literally "sustaining power." Therefore to forget the self is to be sustained, made stable. There is no longer self or other, for self and other are the same. One's body-mind is completely filled with the Dharma. Others' body-minds are also gone, likewise filled with the Dharma. This is what it means to "become one with universal truth."

---

3   Words the infant Buddha is said to have uttered moments after he was born.
4   Karaki Junzō, Ryōkan (Tokyo: Chikuma Shobo, 1971).

The Issue of the Heart

Entering on the path of Buddhism does not mean studying and revering scriptures outside oneself. At issue is the heart. The heart is the target of Buddhism and, as Dōgen saw it, the place where the Buddha resides. This became Ryōkan's view as well. By forsaking everything, he arrived at that state of mind.

Every day in the temple the monks rose at three in the morning to meditate, and it's said that Ryōkan was always first to begin. Here is another affecting poem about his experience in training:

> I remember when I was at Entsūji
> always lamenting that my path was a solitary one.
> Fetching firewood, I would think of Mr. Pang;
> Treading the mortar, I would recall Old Lu.
> At *nisshitsu* I never lagged behind,
> always got to morning meditation first.
> Since I left the temple
> thirty years have slipped by.
> Mountains and seas now intervene, and
> no word comes of those I once knew.
> Remembering all I owe my teacher, I end in tears—
> let them flow, flow on to the river!

Nisshitsu, "entering the room," refers to the private interview between the Zen master, Kokusen, and the student. Pang Jushi (740–808) was a lay Zen adherent in China who made bamboo baskets for a living and carried firewood. Old Lu is Huineng (638–713), the sixth and last patriarch of Chinese Zen, who used to pound rice in the temple. While earnestly devoting himself to his various tasks, Ryōkan felt isolated; the others would go on to have careers as priest or head priest somewhere, while he alone continued to practice the Way single-mindedly. The poem is an unfeigned portrait of the artist as a Zen acolyte.

Unswerving in his commitment, Ryōkan faithfully cast everything aside as instructed. Tanikawa Toshirō, the author of many books on Ryōkan, points out that monks of that era tried to make funerals as imposing as they could, prioritizing outward form to earn their bread and butter. Sōtō Zen monks were no exception; they were expected to play a variety of musical instruments with panache. In their midst, Ryōkan alone focused intently on practicing the Way. Therein lies his greatness.

3

Who Am I?

A Nobody

Having left home at eighteen to become a monk, from age twenty-two to thirty-four Ryōkan trained under Kokusen at Entsūji. When he was thirty-four Kokusen died and Ryōkan left the temple, some say because he didn't get along with the master's successor. For the next five years he wandered about, but apart from a single report of a meeting in Shikoku with someone named Kondō Banjō, his itinerary is unknown.

He returned to Echigo at thirty-nine, but not to his old home. Instead he went to the coastal village of Gōmoto, where he rented a small hut, one used originally for the burning of seaweed to extract salt. He gained permission from local people before moving in. Life must have been difficult at first, as country folk generally don't take kindly to outsiders, but little by little people were drawn to him. When out begging, if he received even a little extra rice, he gave it to the poor or fed it to the birds. He took no more for himself than he needed and led a spiritual life in his hermitage, so gradually he earned people's trust and respect.

When he first left home, Ryōkan turned his back on the privileges, possessions and connections enjoyed by the family of a village headman, and later in life no one came to his aid; he was completely on his own. He could easily have found a position at a temple had he wished, but he abandoned that path as well. He was a monk without any affiliation—a useless nobody, neither a farmer nor a village headman nor a samurai. He did write poetry and do calligraphy, but he never turned professional. He wasn't anything except himself—a human being who knew nothing about the workings of the world and was of no earthly use to anyone. But in his increasing contacts with the ordinary folk around him, he showed a winning warmth of spirit. As we have seen, when he went to stay at the Kera house, the family enjoyed his calming presence. He had that effect on people.

Free and Easy

At some point after Ryōkan's return to Echigo, his poetry took on what he himself called playfulness, a free and easy spirit that became his trademark. Here is an example:

> Can't remember how many years it's been
> since I came to live in this place.
> When worn out, I stretch out my legs and sleep;
> when well, I put on straw sandals and go begging,
> never caring about praise,
> never concerned about scorn.
> My parents gave birth to me,
> so I accept this chance—might as well enjoy my life!

The line "When worn out, I stretch out my legs and sleep" represents what was a truly pleasurable time for Ryōkan. When well, he goes out with his begging bowl. Unlike his years of vagabondage, Ryōkan is now settled in one place, even if it is only a grass hut.

Around the same time, he wrote this *waka*:

kusa no io ni   In my hut of grass,
ashi sashinobete   legs stretched out before me,
koyamada no   listening with joy
sanden no kawazu   to the chorus of frogs
kiku ga tanoshisa   in the mountain paddies.

This too seems nothing special on first reading. It is set in the spring, around May. Since the weather has grown warmer, he is sitting with the window and door open, legs stretched out lazily in his grass hut. Then all he needs to be filled with deep peace and joy is to hear the nearby croaking of frogs. The scene is perfectly ordinary. Frogs are croaking, that's all, and yet it makes his heart sing to think that he and they are welcoming spring's advent together. He feels one with the breathing of the universe. What could be more peaceful, more fulfilling? As in the previous poem, he leaves all to the workings of fate, ready to accept what comes, ready above all to take pleasure in the present moment of being alive.

This next poem is famous for its portrayal of Ryōkan bouncing a ball. This one is a *chōka*, a longer form of *waka*.

fuyugomori haru sarikureba   Winter hibernation over,
ii kou to kusa no iori o   I left my hut, bowl in hand,
tachiidete sato ni ikeba   to beg for rice in the village,
tamahoko no michi no chimata ni   where in the streets
kodomora ga ima o haru be to   children glad of spring
temari tsuku hifumiyoimuna   were bouncing balls, counting
                        1-2-3-4-5-6-7.

na ga tsukeba a wa utai   You bounce and I'll sing,
a ga tsukeba na wa utai   I'll bounce and you sing.

tsukite utaite kasumi tatsu	Bouncing and singing,
nagaki haruhi o kurashitsuru kamo	we passed the long spring day.

Ryōkan wrote many variations on this theme and must have taken special pleasure in such episodes. The coming of spring gladdened him, as did the sight of children at play in the streets. He joined in their games—rare behavior for an adult in those days, or even now for that matter. Being seen at play would have been embarrassing; adults were supposed to get busy doing something useful, not stand around bouncing a ball. But Ryōkan was content to play with the children. Playing, especially with children, was part and parcel of his Zen discipline. To be alive is to take pleasure in the moment, to savor it with joy—even if the townsfolk couldn't see it that way.

kono sato ni	In this village
temari tsukitsutsu	bouncing balls
kodomora to	at play with kids,
asobu haruhi wa	wishing this spring day
kurezu tomo yoshi	would never end.

Nothing made Ryōkan happier than to fritter his time away like this. Joining in the children's play, he felt truly alive.

kasumi tatsu	This long spring day
nagaki haruhi ni	of rising mist
kodomora to	I spend with kids
temari tsukitsutsu	bouncing balls with them
kono hi kurashitsu	the whole day long.

He is relaxed and carefree, utterly self-sufficient. These poems are easy to understand and exude a delightful warmth and fragrance. Unconcerned with the drive to make money or get ahead of the next fellow, Ryōkan is removed from such struggles and living truly from the heart, at peace with himself and with nature. This is the meaning of "playfulness" in his poems.

Who Am I?

Ryōkan was a nobody, but precisely for that reason he was forced constantly to question his identity. Probably no other poet has ever posed the question "Who am I?" so insistently. Certainly in Tokugawa-period Japan no one thought that way. Everyone in society had their role to play, so there was no point in questioning one's identity. But "Who am I?" is at all times the starting point of Ryōkan's poetry. This is so in the next poem, for example, which no one but Ryōkan would ever have dreamed of writing:

What does my life resemble?
Carefree, I leave it all to fate.
Laughable and deplorable,
neither lay nor priest.
In the dreary spring rain
plum blossoms in the garden do not light up my room.
All morning long I sit by the hearth
facing myself without a word.
One hand behind my back, I search my copy-book,
practice calligraphy to relax.

This way of thinking was unique to Ryōkan. First he asks himself what his life is like, and then he proceeds to answer the question.

Other poems show the same pattern. Ryōkan was friends with a Confucian scholar and prominent calligrapher named Kameda Bōsai, who also composed superb *kanshi*. But where Bōsai, serious and erudite, fit the image of a *kanshi* poet, Ryōkan did not. He fit no category, was truly a nobody, as he himself well knew.

> Where has my life come from,
> where will it go?
> Alone I sit by the window in my hut
> in quiet meditation.
> Ponder as I will, I don't know how it all began;
> how can I know how it may end?
> I am as I am.
> In any case, all is emptiness.
> I exist alone in the void;
> how can there be good or evil?
> All I know to do
> is take life as it comes.

The "emptiness" and "void" here are *kū*, as in the fundamental Buddhist formulation *shiki soku ze kū*, "form is emptiness." He feels as if he is floating alone in the void. How can there be any distinction between good and evil? Ryōkan had no interest in dualism. He feels himself alone in total emptiness, no idea what to do. He can only calmly accept whatever comes. As in this poem, Ryōkan was constantly pondering the question of who or what he might be.

To Feel with the Spirit

The English language distinguishes between "mind" and "heart"; the former refers to logical, rational thinking, the latter to emotional thinking. I learned this distinction from my friend Kajima Shōzō (1923–2015), the poet and scholar of English literature. In ordinary daily life, we are immersed in the world of practical matters, always deciding what step to take next. Our minds are constantly busy tackling problems like how to raise production or sales, while our hearts have precious little to do.

Ryōkan wasn't good at matters of the mind, stressing his uselessness over and over. He was all heart. He would direct a penetrating gaze into the deep recesses of his heart, looking always and only at absolute problems, those transcending time and place. From society's point of view he was a good-for-nothing dimwit, a hopeless case—but his heart overflowed with feelings of indescribable refinement and good humor.

Ryōkan describes himself in a variety of ways in his poems. Sometimes he dismisses himself as someone of no consequence: "Some may call me 'a person of no account'–/that's me to a T." Since becoming a Zen monk, he left all to fate, and lived without making any special disposition for himself. He was a mendicant monk, a beggar. People might criticize him for not amounting to anything, and they would be right; no one amounted to less than him. It is a scathing self-assessment. Another poem contains the lines "What does my life resemble?/Languidly, I let time go by." He quietly let life unfold as it would while he passed the time. He also calls himself incorrigibly stupid: "My stubborn foolishness has no like;/I make the trees and grasses my neighbors." Because he is stubborn and foolish, in other words, he avoids the company of others and lives in friendship with trees and grasses. Disinclined to try to tell delusion from enlightenment, he will grow old and feeble, foolish as ever, laughing at himself. Elsewhere, rubbing in how the world sees him, he writes, "Stubborn idiot, when will you die?/A life of lonely poverty." And he calls himself "scarecrow of the mountain paddies."

These judgments may sound harsh, but Ryōkan is not coldly self-mocking; rather, he is grinning at his stubborn foolishness, accepting himself as he is and taking pleasure in his life, willingly yielding to fate. These lines are a total affirmation of his existence.

When Ryōkan received his certificate of enlightenment, his Zen master, Kokusen, composed a verse to commemorate the occasion, dedicating it to "Ryōkan the hermitage master."

> Ryōkan looks foolish, but the way in his heart is wide.
> Free of care, he leaves all to fate. Who can see his wisdom?
> I hereby give him my rattan staff, knowing that
> wherever he goes, he'll be sure to nap at his ease.

Ryōkan was one of Kokusen's oldest disciples, and had been given a hermitage to live in. In this poem Kokusen praises the level of understanding Ryōkan has reached, and gives him the staff as an emblem of his having achieved enlightenment, predicting that wherever he takes the staff in his peregrinations, he is sure to be at ease and take plenty of naps. The poem conveys both respect and affection, and it effectively sums up who Ryōkan was.

4

Compassionate by Nature

What It Means to Be Alive

Though Ryōkan had no place in the world of reason and set no store by
it, living rather from the heart, he was steeped not just in Buddhist scriptures and ancient Japanese writings but also in Chinese classics, including the *Analects* of Confucius as well as the Daoist teachings of Laozi and
Zhuangzi, which he absorbed and reflected in his life. The following passage by Laozi reads like a description of Ryōkan:

> Others are clear and bright, while I alone am lackluster and faint.
> Others are clever and sharp, while I alone am foggy. I rock like the
> waves of the sea and sough like the restless wind. Others all serve
> a purpose, but I alone am inflexible and incompetent. I am not like
> others. I value being nourished by the great mother, the Way.[5]

This is him to the core. He served no purpose in society, but those he came
into contact with were left purer, more honest and cheerful, and full of the

---

5   Kanaya Osamu, *Rōshi*, Chapter 20 (Tokyo: Kodansha Gakujutsu Bunko, 1997). Translated
    from the Japanese.

joy of living. When he went to live in his mountain hut, people were leery of him at first but gradually came to appreciate his true value—beginning with the children.

I have already introduced his *chōka* on bouncing balls with children, and there is a long Chinese poem on the same topic that shows clearly the warm relationship he enjoyed with them. It is a delightful poem, a personal favorite of mine.

> Green spring, the start of the second month,
> colors of things turning fresh and new.
> Now I take my begging bowl,
> in high spirits set out for town.
> Little children quickly spot me,
> happily flock around.
> They drag me to the temple gate,
> swarming so my steps are slow.
> I set my bowl on a white rock,
> hang my alms-bag on a green branch.
> Here we wrestle on a hundred grasses,
> over here we kick balls in the air.
> While I kick, they sing, and
> while I sing, they do the kicking.
> Going and coming, we kick the ball,
> unaware of the passage of time.
> Passers-by turn to look at me and laugh,
> "What makes you act this way?"
> I shake my head, not answering—
> even if I could explain, what would be the point?
> You want to know what's in my heart?
> All along, just this, only this!

Ryōkan inhabits a world which those who understand, understand, and those who don't, don't. Therefore, what's the use of trying to explain? He throws himself heart and soul into playing with the children, forgetting all else: this is how to live in harmony with the Buddha Way. Listening to birdsong and otherwise enjoying nature is part of being alive, as is playing with children; therein lies the most profound and true way of living, he says. But people whose minds are preoccupied with making things, plowing fields, and earning a living fail to understand. Therefore, words and knowledge are of no use in expressing his world. The fundamental, absolute essence of what it means to be human is inexpressible. One must be spiritually awakened to grasp it. Knowing this, Ryōkan only hangs his head and doesn't answer when people ask him what on earth he's doing. The children, however, are fully aware of his purity of spirit and intention.

Healing and Consolation

Someone with great understanding of Ryōkan was Harada Arinori, a physician and wealthy landowner who studied alongside him in Ōmori Shiyō's school. Harada was a man of learning, proficient in both *waka* and *kanshi*, as was his son Shōtei. After Shōtei's son died in a smallpox epidemic, Ryōkan wrote a poem of mourning with this preface: "Last year many children were lost to smallpox. I wrote this poem on behalf of their broken-hearted parents."

azusa yumi	Catalpa-bowed
haru mo haru to mo	spring does not seem like
omooezu	spring at all
suginishi kora ga	when I remember them,
koto o omoeba	the children who are gone.

"Catalpa-bowed" is an archaic *makurakotoba* ("pillow-word") associated
with spring. The poem needs no other explanation. Simple and heartfelt, it
straightforwardly conveys the emotions of bereft parents.

The following poems are similar:

hito no ko no	At the sight of
asobu o mireba	other people's children
niwatazumi	absorbed in play
nagaruru namida	my tears fall thick and fast,
todomekanetsumo	no way to stop them.

mono omoi	When my thoughts
subenaki toki wa	are too painful to bear
uchiidete	I go out and
furuno ni ouru	pick shepherd's purse
nazuna o zo tsumu	growing in the fields.

Visiting fields where the vanished children used to play, he finds comfort
in picking shepherd's purse in their stead. Poems like these must have
been a great consolation to bereaved parents. Though he had no other role
in society, Ryōkan took it upon himself to heal broken hearts and console
those in mourning through his poetry.

Another landowner in a village near Gogō-an, Ryōkan's hermitage, was
the saké brewer Abe Sadayoshi. A great fan of Ryōkan's, Sadayoshi would
often call on him bearing gifts of saké and food. As an amateur poet keen
on poetry, he enjoyed exchanging *waka* with his friend. Once he brought
over some saké and presented it with this verse: "Bearing soup and saké,
across the rugged mountain I have come to try your radishes." Here is
Ryōkan's reply:

ashihiki no	You are welcome
Kugami no yama no	to these radishes I planted
yamabata ni	in the field
makishi ōne o	on rugged Mt. Kugami—
asazu ose kimi	help yourself, take all you want!

Like Sadayoshi, Ryōkan uses *ashihiki* (literally, "foot-dragging"; rugged), the archaic pillow-word, or conventional epithet, for mountains. The diction in the last line is also taken from an ancient ballad. He was able to come up with such lines on the spur of the moment. The poem is gracious and genial.

Another time in the fall Sadayoshi came to visit, and as they amused themselves exchanging verses, before they knew it night came on and Sadayoshi stood up to leave. Ryōkan presented him with this poem in parting:

tsuki yomi no	Wait for
hikari o machite	the light of the moon
kaerimase	before you go:
yamaji wa kuri no	mountain paths are strewn
iga no ōki ni	with chestnut burrs.

Again, the poem is straightforward, simply presenting the situation, but it is alive with concern for his friend and desire to have him linger. The modern poet Yoshino Hideo has declared this to be one of Ryōkan's finest works: "It reads seamlessly. The first half implies his desire to have his friend stay even a little longer, and the second half expresses concern for his friend's safety; the combination of these finely tuned emotions is moving."[6] With great simplicity, the poem conveys human warmth.

---

6   Yoshino Hideo, *Ryōkan* (Tokyo; Art Days, 2001).

Ryōkan and Abe Sadayoshi exchanged a great many poems, a testament to the depth of their friendship.

Falling Under His Spell

We have seen that wealthy landowners, children, and literati like Abe Sadayoshi enjoyed strong bonds with Ryōkan, but that's not all. Even the local farmers came to trust him. They spoke his name with respect and valued his company. This closeness is reflected in the following Chinese poem.

Going and going, I wind up deep in the countryside
just at eventide.
Sparrows gather in bamboo groves,
twittering noisily as they fly about.
An old farmer heading home, carrying his spade,
sees me and greets me like an old friend.
Calling to his wife, he offers me some home brew
and boiled vegetables picked nearby.
Sitting face to face we drink,
talking and laughing—how strange!
Pleasantly drunk together,
unconcerned with right and wrong.

The last line means that the two men are above simplistic dualism and concerned with more important matters, mainly that of being alive. The affection between them shines through clearly. The farmer in question was surely illiterate, but Ryōkan formed a strong friendship with him and others like him.

I am reminded of this wonderful quotation from "One-sheet Document," a summation of the essential teachings of Hōnen, the medieval founder of

Pure Land Buddhism in Japan: "However intensely one may have studied all the Buddhist scriptures, act like a simple-minded illiterate or an ignorant monk or nun, never assuming an air of pedantry and only reciting the *nembutsu*." The *nembutsu* is Namu Amida Butsu, the invocation of Amida Buddha's name. Hōnen himself actually did study all the Buddhist scriptures. He spread the teaching that salvation comes through simple recitation of the *nembutsu*, but at the same time he was a man of extraordinary learning, matchless in debate. His scholarly attainments make this admonition all the more telling. He holds up as a model someone who has deep learning yet humbly casts it aside, "only reciting the *nembutsu*."

Ryōkan was just such a man. Extraordinarily well-read, he was easily one of the leading intellectuals of his day. He taught himself to read *man'yōgana*, the difficult writing system used to record the poems in the *Man'yōshū* (*Collection of Ten Thousand Leaves*), and immersed himself in the book, learning much of it by heart. Fond of Tang-dynasty poetry by Hanshan and others, he himself wrote superb poems in Chinese and was moreover an outstanding calligrapher. Despite all this, he abandoned everything to live in a grass hut, drinking home-brewed saké with farmers and enjoying heart-to-heart conversations with them as their equal. Lacking intellectual pretensions, he reached out to others with sincerity.

Ryōkan's one religious disciple was a layman named Miwa Saichi who lived in Yoita, Echigo. On a hilltop there I once visited the Miwa family grave and found it old, small, and unadorned. Saichi's sudden death in 1807, when Ryōkan was fifty years old, came as a great blow. The following *waka* gives some indication of the affection the master bore his disciple; it could even pass for a love poem.

kono sato no	In this village
ikiki no hito wa	so many people
amata aredo	come and go,

kimi shi nakereba	but without you
sabishikari keri	it is lonely.

There is a nearly identical *sedōka* (poem in six lines in a repeating pattern of 5-7-7) on the same theme, using more archaic language. *Sasu take no*, "erect as a bamboo stalk," is a pillow-word used with members of the nobility.

kono sato ni	In this village
ikiki no hito wa	many are the people
sa wa ni aredomo	who come and go
sasu take no	but without you
kimi shi masaneba	erect as a bamboo stalk
sabishikari keri	it is lonely.

All of Ryōkan's *sedōka* are fine, and this one I think conveys the depth of his emotion even better than the *waka*. Both poems emphasize the emptiness he felt on losing someone he cherished. Clearly Saichi meant a great deal to him.

5

A Man of Inaction

The Dao: A World that Is Absolute

As I have stressed, Ryōkan operated not by the dictates of the mind or intellect but by those of the heart. This point is key. People of mental acumen are useful in the day-to-day business of society—production, sales, current profits and losses, opening markets, speculation—as well as in handing down verdicts. Society has many such experts, and yet overreliance on intellect can impair judgment, leading for example to mistakes in the handling of nuclear fuel and other serious problems: Japan's highways were said to be earthquake-proof, yet they collapsed in the Kobe earthquake of 1995. Ryōkan was not at all bound by the world of the intellect. As Hōnen advised, he lived like a "simple-minded illiterate." He was a profoundly simple man.

The ancient Chinese sage Laozi offered similar advice. Ryōkan was well versed in the teachings of Laozi and Zhuangzi, and lived in their spirit. Laozi's words are extremely difficult; what follows is Kanaya Osamu's rendering of a section of chapter 48 in *The Way and Its Power*.

Devote yourself to learning and your knowledge will increase day by day; devote yourself to the Way and day by day your knowledge will decrease. Decrease it all the more until you arrive at the point of inaction, where no special actions are taken. Remain thus inactive and you will be able to accomplish all things well.[7]

This is paradoxical. It is a matter of simple arithmetic that learning more day by day will increase one's store of knowledge, but knowledgeable people tend to take pride in their knowledge and be blinded by it. Those who follow the Way—those who live by the dictates of the heart—cast aside their knowledge, however great, day by day. The Way is a world of non-discernment, a world where discernment is beside the point; the Way is indivisible, the fountainhead of all things, absolute. Or it could be called one's true self, the self in the innermost recesses of the heart. Those who live in the Way continually strip away their knowledge, depleting their store until nothing remains. Then they enter the realm of what Laozi calls "inaction," where the heart is free, unrestricted by notions of right and wrong. At this point, strange to say, the education one has cast aside comes into play as needed, and the intellect assumes its proper role. This is why, says Laozi, he who enters the realm of inaction and remains there can do all things well.

Beyond Duality

If ever there was a man of inaction, Ryōkan was that man. Never in his life did he do anything of the slightest use to society. He was not bound by intellect or by religious teachings. He studied Zen but respected all forms of Buddhism, honoring the *nembutsu* as well as the Lotus Sutra. Many of his poems deny the significance of dualistic thinking.

7　Kanaya, *op. cit.*, Chapter 48.

People in this world
are like plants of every variety.
Each clings to his view,
insisting he is right.
Resemble me and your wrong is right,
differ from me and your right is wrong.
Only what *I* think right is right;
what others find wrong I ignore.
Each person judges on his own,
but the true way was never so narrow.
With a pole they seek to fathom the ocean,
revealing their foolishness.

For Ryōkan this poem is unusually argumentative, but it represents a fundamental conviction.

Zen Buddhism itself rejects a dualistic, right-versus-wrong approach to life. Zen seeks to return to a non-dualistic world, one that is not relativistic but absolute, and that is where Ryōkan stands. Even in our time, in their zeal to promote their position, people tend to grant credence to any view favorable to theirs and dismiss all others as wrongheaded. This tendency is widespread, and nowhere more so than in the world of politics. It's the same with aesthetic judgments; as Laozi said, there is ugliness because there is beauty.

Here is a poem giving Ryōkan's take on the matter:

There is beauty, and so there is ugliness;
there is right, and so there is wrong.
Erudition and ignorance are relative;
delusion and enlightenment go hand in hand.
This is how it has always been;

it's nothing new.
Striving to give up this and grab that—
all of it utter foolishness.
What's strange is this:
Everyone focuses on what fluctuates.

Ryōkan wrote five or six poems on dualism, so the topic clearly weighed on his mind.

Laozi disliked differentiating between right and wrong as much as Ryōkan did, which probably helps explain why Ryōkan was so fond of his teachings and those of Zhuangzi. Laozi said this: "What society speaks of as goodness or beauty is imprecise, and it is wrong to be too caught up in such things. Having and not-having each arise from the other, having from not-having and not-having from having."[8] He went on to declare that difficult and easy, long and short, high and low, front and back, beautiful and ugly are all relative, each pole defined by and dependent on its opposite. That is why anyone who would follow the Dao, or Way, must adopt a stance of inaction and observe the teaching of silence, to avoid letting distinctions among words and concepts distance him or her from truth. This is precisely what Ryōkan is getting at in his poem. Truth lies beyond artificial distinctions such as beautiful and ugly, good and bad.

Want Nothing and Be Satisfied with Everything

Since Ryōkan lived this way, when people came to him for advice he responded "like a fool" and imparted no wisdom. As one who did not

---

8   Kanaya, *op cit.*, Chapter 2.

believe in absolute beauty or goodness, he had no interest in handing down decisions or ultimatums.

Ryōkan's younger brother had a son named Yasuki who took to drinking and idleness; no one could talk sense into him. He made no effort to mend his ways and turned a deaf ear to all advice. Yasuki's mother came and begged Ryōkan to give the boy a good talking-to. Ryōkan obediently went to their house and stayed three nights, but when the mother looked furtively in on them, she found he wasn't scolding her son at all. Finally, just as he was about to leave, Ryōkan asked Yasuki to tie up his straw sandals. Yasuki was puzzled by the request but, glad to have escaped a lecture, did so with pleasure. Then he felt something cold fall on him. He looked up and saw that Ryōkan's eyes were full of tears. The realization that his uncle was shedding tears on his behalf did more for him than any scolding could have done.

This story is revealing. As Ryōkan well knew, exchanges of opinion inevitably involve clashes over who is right. No matter how worthy someone's opinion may be, someone with an opposing opinion will be inclined to dismiss it out of hand. Knowing this, Ryōkan avoided pronouncements about right and wrong. He stayed away from dualistic, judgmental thinking and simply showed total, heartfelt concern for the other person. Laozi's philosophy of inaction, through which one exerts a profound influence despite—or by—doing nothing, exactly describes Ryōkan's approach in this story.

Ryōkan was free of wants. Wanting things inevitably leads to distinctions of right and wrong, so harboring desire is to be avoided. Ryōkan wrote the following poem about eradicating desire:

Want nothing, and be satisfied with everything;
seek something, and there is never enough.
Simple greens can satisfy hunger;

a plain robe is enough to cover one.
I walk alone and befriend deer,
chant poems and sing with village kids.
Wash out my ears with water by a rock
and enjoy the soughing of wind in a clifftop pine.

Ryōkan has painted a picture of himself. He ate poorly, but whatever he received in his begging bowl enabled him to stave off starvation. He owned only a black monk's robe, but it was enough to keep him warm. Not wanting anything more, he was always perfectly satisfied with what he had. He befriended deer on solitary walks, wrote poems and recited them in a loud voice when no one was around, sang songs with local children. When he heard something unpleasant, like Chinese sages of old he would wash out his ears with pure water, then listen with relish to the wind in a clifftop pine. His solitary walks and habit of reciting poetry aloud show elevation of mind. The first two lines aptly sum up Ryōkan's approach to life. Till the day he died, he lived in a rough hermitage with next to nothing to his name.

The desire to own things knows no bounds. Still not enough, we tell ourselves, and seek yet more. The more we have, the more we want, as if by the act of filling our stomachs we starve. A prime example is Japan's period of high economic growth toward the end of the twentieth century. There is no clearer example of what happens when people are ruled by their desires. Companies produced new product after new product, advertising them with clever commercials. People bought up all the products, whether televisions or cars, wristwatches or cameras. Everything new seemed fine. The entire country was in a fever to work hard to earn money and buy, buy, buy. Then the economic bubble burst, and it finally dawned on us that things, however many we may acquire, do not bring happiness. Ryōkan's words are simple, but they drive home a message that modern Japanese people need to hear. Let us hope that the twenty-first century doesn't bring more foolish greed such as we exhibited in the latter half of the twentieth century. If you would be happy, you must cast aside your desires and live on a spiritual plane. Ryōkan was absolutely right.

Happiness Piled on Happiness

Now it's time for me to introduce what is held to be Ryōkan's most representative poem:

All my life, too lazy to make something of myself.
I leave all to nature.
In my alms-sack, three measures of rice,
by the hearth one bundle of firewood.
Why ask who's enlightened and who's not?
What do I know of mere dust, fame and riches?
Rainy nights in my grass hut
I stick out my two legs as I please.

Here is an expanded paraphrase: Looking back on my life, although I was born and went out into the world, I grew sick of living in an environment where people elbow others aside to get ahead in the struggle for success. Fed up with that sort of life, I let my fate unfold as it would. Now the three measures of rice I gained by begging are in my alms-sack, and next to the sunken hearth is a bundle of sticks I gathered for firewood. What more do I need? This is plenty. I've lost interest in questions of delusion or enlightenment, the world of discrimination where people debate right and wrong. Desire for fame and riches means nothing to me. On rainy nights in my simple thatched hut I can hear the patter of raindrops. Sitting listening with my legs stretched out any old way—this is my greatest pleasure.

What could be simpler than this definition of happiness: stretching out legs tired from a day of begging? What the average person would regard as of no consequence brings Ryōkan extraordinary happiness, since he is penniless to begin with and completely unencumbered. I can't help feeling that this poem contains a vital clue to a happy life. People do not become content by adding more and more to the sum of their possessions, feeding their desires. The more money they have, the more they want. The more things they own, the more they crave. This has been called the "age of satiety"; a person who is surrounded by food of every variety and constantly eating, never hungry, will never know what it is to taste something truly delicious. Hunger teaches us the real value and flavor of food. The same principle holds true in other areas of life. Only when we deny ourselves and seek to live without desire can we savor the preciousness and joy of life.

Ryōkan's poetry draws on his life to illustrate this idea. All of his poetry, in Japanese and Chinese alike, is in this mode. Things that most people would find trivial brought him joy. He devoted himself to living this way. Here is another poem in the same vein, also a self-portrait:

As a boy I tossed aside brush and inkstone,
privately admired those who led a monastic life.
Carrying flask and begging-bowl,
how many springs did I roam?
Returning home, I lived under a cliff
in a grass hut, a life of quiet poverty.
I listen to birdsong, finer than any music;
look at the clouds and make them my friend.
Below the rock is a pure spring
where I can wash my robe and cloth;
atop the cliff are pines and oaks,
their dry branches a source of firewood.

Happiness piled on happiness:
savor this time forever.

When Ryōkan studied at the school run by Ōmori Shiyō, he was, at one point, prepared to make his living as a scholar, but gave up the idea while still a young man. His admiration for pure-hearted people who had taken religious vows grew until he did the same. For years he wandered the land with the bare necessities—a flask and a begging-bowl—and no more. After living as a vagabond, he returned home to take up an impoverished life in a hut under a cliff, listening to the sweet music of birds and looking at the clouds, making them his friend. A spring supplied water for his laundry needs; hilltop trees, pine and oak, supplied twigs and branches for his fire-wood. Poor though he was, he was content with his life and grateful; he could not have asked for anything more.

Yoshida Kenkō

c. 1283–c. 1353

Kano Tan'yū, *Portrait of the Monk Kenkō* (detail), Kanagawa

Yoshida Kenkō

A poet and essayist. His lay name was Urabe Kaneyoshi. At a young age he became house steward of the Horikawa family and served at court as chamberlain. Around age 30 he became a monk and took up a life of seclusion. He is counted among the four masters of the conservative Nijō school of poetry, along with Tonna, Keiun, and Jōben. In his philosophical miscellany *Essays in Idleness* he reveals superlative abilities as a thinker and critic.

6

The Joy of Living

If We Hate Death, We Should Love Life

Essays in Idleness by the monk Yoshida Kenkō can be summed up as an explanation of how to live well. The content is varied, however, and can take on an entirely different cast depending on the section chosen. I would like to begin by taking up sections having to do with death.

In the latter half of section 93, we find these words: "If we hate death, we should love life. Let us take pleasure in the joy of living day by day." The meaning is clear. Hating death obliges us to love life. Life is too precious not to savor the joy of living each day.

Years ago when I came upon these lines, I felt as if they floated up from the rest of the page and shone with a special light. I sensed in them the radiance of life, and ever after they have been the foundation of my own musings about life and death. As I say the words over to myself like an incantation, the philosophy they express has put down such roots inside me that I now feel as if I own them. No classic of any place or time sums up with such admirable concision the relationship between life and death for living human beings.

"Someone was selling an ox. A buyer offered to pay the asking price and take possession the following day, but during the night the ox died. The buyer profited, and the seller suffered a loss." Someone told this story.

A bystander commented, "The owner of the ox may have suffered a loss, but he also profited greatly. The reason is that those who are alive are unaware of the nearness of death. The ox was unaware, and so was the man. The ox unexpectedly died, and its owner unexpectedly lived. One day of life weighs more than ten thousand pieces of gold, while the value of the ox was lighter than a goose feather. Someone who gains ten thousand pieces of gold and loses a penny cannot be said to have suffered a loss."

Everyone scoffed and protested, "That logic doesn't apply only to the owner of the ox!"

The bystander replied, "If we hate death, we should love life. Let us take pleasure in the joy of living day by day."

We can assume that the bystander is Kenkō himself. I think this passage is saying that without a clear view of death, we cannot have a clear view of life or feel any love of life.

This observation may seem obvious, and yet over the past forty-odd years Japan has gradually lost sight of death. Television and other mass media promote the tendency to think that life must be at all times cheerful, young, and pleasant, that there must be nothing dark, depressing, senescent, or sad. Since death is the darkest and saddest of all things, for a long time no one looked it in the face. During Japan's period of high economic growth in particular, death was taboo.

Death in Modern Times

Death used to be something close at hand. In my own memory, before the war those who fell sick seldom saw a doctor or went into the hospital. A sick family member would be given a room in the house or, if no such room was available, the sickbed would be screened off. Everyone would tiptoe around and do what they could to help bring about a quick recovery. Then at some point families stopped providing care and instead had sick relatives go into the hospital. Certainly the lack of space in Japanese homes is a factor, along with the nuclearization of families, which leaves no one to be a full-time caregiver. In any case, hospitalizing the sick has become the norm. Caregiving is no longer done by families in the home but by professionals in the hospital.

What does this mean? To the caregiver, the sick person is no longer a family member, a living human being, but a patient, someone defined by illness. Curing the illness is therefore the paramount concern. The patient is treated not as a human being but as an ailing body, and the medical staff are invested with full authority. Family members are not made privy to all vital information but leave everything in the doctor's hands. If the illness is terminal, the doctor's focus is not on the emotional state of a person who must come to grips with his or her impending death but on medical technology—the progression of the illness and corresponding options for treatment: "The illness is currently at thus-and-such stage, so thus-and-such treatment must be done." The patient cannot contemplate his or her own death, however imminent, because the doctor speaks entirely in terms of the appropriate manner of treatment every step of the way.

Nowadays it has become commonplace to let someone know that they have cancer, but not long ago in Japan nondisclosure of a cancer diagnosis was the norm, and many people died never knowing they had a terminal disease. This disturbing attempt to shut out death arose during the period of high economic growth following World War II.

In the early 1980s, French historian Philippe Ariès wrote a brilliant survey of Western attitudes toward death from medieval times through the present. In it, he points out that twentieth-century attitudes toward human death underwent a fundamental change.

The intent now is to shield from the pain and sordidness of death not the one who is dying but those around him or her—society itself—and to spare them the consternation and unbearably strong distress evoked by death's intrusion in the midst of their otherwise happy lives. This is because it is now accepted that life must always be, or appear to be, happy.[9]

In other words, the modern approach to death is concerned less with the dying individual and more with how to soften the impact of death on the living.

Looking open-eyed at death is no longer done. In medieval Europe, the house gates would be opened when someone was dying so that various people could gather around the deathbed to say their goodbyes. The one dying would express thanks before exiting this life. That's how people used to do it, but not anymore. Today someone who becomes ill dies not at home in the company of loved ones but alone in a hospital bed. Hospitals are where one goes to die. Initiative in end-of-life matters has been wrested not only from the one dying but from the family as well, and now lies firmly in the hands of doctors and nursing staff.

---

9 Itō Akira and Naruse Komao, trans. *Shi to rekishi* (Tokyo: Misuzu Shobo, 1983). Translated from the Japanese.

"Death has retreated," says Ariès. "It has left the home and transferred to the hospital. It is no longer present in our ordinary, familiar world. Because people today have little chance to view death close at hand, they have forgotten all about it."[10]

In Japan today, it is certainly correct to say that death has retreated to hospitals and made itself all but invisible. Death-related matters are relegated to doctors, who make judgment calls regarding what medical technology to use. In an encouraging reaction against such medical despotism, more people have begun demanding "death with dignity." After former US ambassador to Japan Edwin O. Reischauer asked that no heroic measures be taken to prolong his life, his wife Haru respected his wishes and he died a natural death. Such cases are on the rise.

Since its foundation in 1976, the Japan Society for Dying with Dignity has spearheaded the movement to allow people to regain control over how they choose to die. Hasegawa Machiko, creator of the long-running comic strip *Sazae-san*, was one of the first Japanese to opt for this manner of dying. She made her sister Mariko promise ahead of time that if she became ill she wouldn't be hospitalized, and when the time came, she took to her bed and died at home. Her death wasn't announced immediately, either, but only after an interval of about a month. There have been many such people. The prolific actress Sawamura Sadako is another, and actor Atsumi Kiyoshi of "Tora-san"[11] fame yet another. Slowly the movement to regain control over one's death is gaining strength in Japan.

---

10 *Ibid.*
11 The film series *Otoko wa tsurai yo* (It's tough being a man), with a Guinness-record-setting 48 installments, starred Atsumi Kiyoshi (1928–1996) as Tora-san, a lovable tramp perennially unlucky in love.

Looking Death in the Eye

That's not all that has changed. For a long time, books about death were taboo in Japan's publishing world, but in the last ten years or so there has been a surge in books dealing with death and aging, some of which I will take up here.

Returning to section 93 of *Essays in Idleness*, the words seem to shine all the more brightly. If we despise death, we must look squarely at it and by so doing intensify our love of life: this is the joy of living of which Kenkō speaks. The love of life requires constant awareness of death.

The foolish man forgets this pleasure and seeks others in vain. Forgetting this treasure and coveting others cannot lead to fulfillment. Failing to enjoy life while you are alive and then fearing death once it draws near makes no sense. The reason people fail to enjoy life is because they have no fear of death. Or rather, it is not that they have no fear of death but that they forget its nearness.

Looking death in the eye heightens the awareness of being alive: herein lies the great paradox of life and death. The modern tendency to conceal death, to render it invisible and exclude it from daily living, ends in our losing sight of the value of life. In the old days, funerals were conducted at home, but nowadays they are generally held at some sort of hall. The remains of the deceased are transported directly from the hospital to the funeral hall, where matters proceed in a ritualized manner at the bidding of the funeral staff and priest. There is little opportunity for people to express grief over death in a personal way. This forced inhibition leads to blindness regarding life.

It may seem paradoxical that facing up to death should give radiance to one's moment-to-moment life, but diaries kept by people suffering from terminal cancer often make just that point. Twentieth-century novelist

Takami Jun contracted esophageal cancer and as the end drew near turned from prose to poetry. His poems were published in a collection entitled *From the Abyss of Death*, his final literary work. Here is one of them, entitled "Outside the Train Window":

Outside the train window is a world
filled with light
filled with joy
vibrantly alive.
When I realize I must part from it,
scenery so familiar
is all at once new.
Human beings and all nature
overflow with joy,
yet I must die.
And yet the world seems so happy.
The knowledge doesn't sadden me
but rather brings comfort.
My heart swells.
A lump fills my chest, tears threaten to spill.[12]

The outside world, indifferent to the imminence of the poet's death, is full of resounding joy—a realization that might seem depressing but that he finds comforting and so inspiring that "tears threaten to spill." How mysterious!

Journalist and social commentator Yanagida Kunio quotes this poem in his book *A Prologue to "Medicine for Dying,"* a record of the struggle with cancer of psychiatrist Nishikawa Kisaku. He adds this comment:

---

12 Takami Jun, *Shi no fuchi yori* (Tokyo: Kodansha Bungei Bunko, 1993).

Awareness of the inevitability of death, whether it be one year away or three, creates circumstances in which one cannot help becoming strongly aware of the "now" of life. Each passing day is highly charged. One feels driven. That tension hones one's sensitivity, making it scores of times keener than before. Light makes a powerful impression and touches the heart, a sure indication of exalted sensitivity.[13]

When one's remaining time is short, life condenses, becomes denser and richer. With each passing moment, one thinks, "I am here now, alive; this person alive here and now is me." This intense sensation of being alive can keep one from falling into despair and instead bring on a state of exaltation, as Yanagida's comments show.

In the words of Yoshida Kenkō, "When a man knows that death is near and inescapable, then for the first time he knows the pleasure of life." Herein lies the mystery of the human heart or soul. Kenkō also wrote,

"The reason people fail to enjoy life is because they have no fear of death. Or rather, it is not that they have no fear of death but that they forget its nearness. One who rises above life and death may be said to have obtained ultimate truth." When the bystander said this, people scoffed all the more.

The thought of perishing is dreadful, but someone who tries to forget or avoid thinking about it only ends up distancing himself from life. Confronting death squarely and preparing for it makes life radiant. This too is paradoxical, but I feel that hidden in this paradox is the secret of joyous living.

"There is no pleasure without pain," we hear. Pain is the necessary condition for the experience of pleasure. Precisely because Ryōkan lived in a

---

13 Yanagida Kunio, "*Shi no igaku*" e no joshō (Tokyo: Shincho Bunko, 1990).

thatched hut with no heating but his hearth, shivering in the cold of winter in meager bedding, he felt enormous delight at the coming of spring. Today we dread suffering and do all we can to avoid it, intent on finding pleasure, but in so doing we miss out on the chance to experience life's true joy. Yoshida Kenkō's *Essays in Idleness* sounds warnings that we need to heed.

Section 137 contains the lines, "Even the young and strong encounter death unexpectedly. It is strange and wonderful to think that one has so far avoided dying." And in section 155 Kenkō writes,

> The hour of death does not await its proper turn. Death does not come at one from the front, but from behind. Everyone knows that death will come; we wait for a death that does not come right away but appears when we least expect it. It is like when the tidal flats extend far before you, while the tide is coming in from the shore behind.

Death, in other words, doesn't come in one-two-three order. It doesn't approach gradually from the front but sneaks up on you invisibly from behind. We all know that we are certain to die, but death comes out of nowhere when we least expect it, and sooner than we think. We are indeed like someone standing in a tidal flat with dry land spreading before him, thinking that it's a long time before the tide comes in—only to find the water lapping right behind him.

This is the heart of the teaching in *Essays in Idleness*. Since death doesn't approach us gradually, head-on, but sneaks up suddenly from behind, even the young and strong must be aware of death and, through their awareness, love life. "Let us take pleasure in the joy of living day by day." I have a feeling that these words urging us to open our eyes to the reality of death are more needed today than ever before.

7

Tranquil in Body and Mind

We Know Not When Death May Come

Essays in Idleness contains many other passages urging us to be aware of death. Here is one from section 108:

> A person of the Way should not be concerned about far-off times. He should only be concerned if this very moment passes by meaninglessly. If someone came and informed me that my life would definitely end tomorrow, what would I turn to for support during the remainder of today, and what would I do? This day that we are alive is indeed that very time. We lose time each day eating, drinking, relieving ourselves, sleeping, talking, and walking around. Little is left over, yet we do and say useless things and think useless thoughts, wasting our time. Not only that, we live our lives wasting days and months, and this is the most foolish thing of all.

A "person of the Way" means someone who has received Buddhist enlightenment, or someone who is undergoing spiritual training in Buddhism. Such a person should not imagine that his or her life lies somewhere far down the road but realize that the present moment, the here and now of life, is all there is, and take care not to let it pass meaninglessly by. It's wasteful to think only of what lies ahead and not devote all one's energy to living here and now.

What if someone came and told me that my life would end tomorrow? What should I rely on for the rest of today; what should I do? In fact, we are always in the position of someone being told that his life will end tomorrow. We need to keep that possibility constantly in mind. Even the young and the strong cannot say when they may die. Since no one knows when death may come, be grateful and astonished that you have escaped so far.

The Happiness of the Soul Facing Death

Kenkō thinks that an awareness of death can heighten our appreciation of life and help us rejoice and take pleasure in being alive. As I embraced his way of thinking, over and over I came to see this phenomenon actually occurring around me.

Take the case of novelist Ozaki Kazuo, whom I think of privately as my mentor. In 1944, after vomiting an alarming amount of blood and nearly dying, he moved from Tokyo to his hometown to recuperate. Friends who went to see him, including fellow writers Nakano Shigeharu and Kambayashi Akatsuki, reported with one voice that he seemed not long for this earth, and his doctor agreed that he had little time left. Ozaki and his family steeled themselves for the inevitable. But Ozaki, being Ozaki, decided to make the most of his remaining time. With the goal of extending his life by five years, he composed a "Five-Year Survival Plan"—the title a humorous takeoff on the habitual pronouncement of five-year economic plans in the USSR and other socialist countries at the time. During what he thought would be his final five years, his very fragility enabled him to observe other life forms with enhanced clarity. Unable to get around, he made meticulous observations of tiny lives close at hand—a spider in the bathroom window, bugs in the garden. "They're alive too. Just like me, these tiny beings are full of life." His ruminations are included in his classic short story "The Beautiful View from the Cemetery." Here is how he describes what it felt like to recover enough to get out of bed, go out onto the veranda, and see the sunshine in his garden. The character Ogata is Ozaki himself.

Early afternoon hours on calm, sunny days were Ogata's happy time. On such days, there was no danger of his having a seizure, and he could raise his voice without experiencing any chest discomfort or breathlessness. He reverted naturally to his usual loud voice.

Ogata would leave his bed and go out onto the veranda, light a cigarette, and lazily blow smoke up into the gentle sunshine. He gazed intently at the shrubs and grasses at the front of the garden, now putting out new leaves with furious energy. "I am alive, I am here": this thought filled him with a jolt of supreme happiness. And at such times everything that touched his heart, everything that met his gaze, became the object of a wan, yet ineradicable, reluctance to bid farewell.

I am so fond of this passage, which I feel expresses the pulse of life in well-crafted prose, that by now I can practically recite it from memory. I feel much the same way when I sit in my garden with my dogs in wintertime and soak up sunshine, as camellia leaves dazzle and birds fly down to the pond for a drink. "I am alive, I am here." These simple words convey the joy of life more directly than any other words I know. This is exactly what Yoshida Kenkō refers to as "the joy of still being alive."

Awareness of such happiness is deepened and made all the sweeter after having fallen ill and lived for a time in expectation of death. Until his illness Ozaki Kazuo lived a fast and dissolute life; if he had stayed physically strong and continued to live that way, he might never have discovered the kind of happiness portrayed here.

Let me offer one more example. The novelist Ōoka Shōhei, someone else whom I secretly revere as my teacher, was drafted in 1944 at thirty-five and sent to the Philippines. Conscripts were generally around twenty years old, but as the Pacific War wore on the prospect of defeat loomed large. By 1943 so many young soldiers had died that the country called on its "old soldiers" to serve. My older brother, whose health was frail, had received a deferment and would normally have been exempt, but despite his poor health and his status as a husband and father he was sent at the age of twenty-seven to Burma, where he died in the battle of Imphal. The drafting of Ōoka, a thirty-five-year-old father of two, was even more irregular, but it happened.

He was sent to the southern front in the Philippines, a battleground from which no one, it was said, could hope to return alive—and indeed, 99 percent of Ōoka's comrades died. Surely no experience could impress one as strongly with the nearness of death. At least their transport ship did manage to hobble into port in Manila without being sunk by an American submarine on the way. Here Ōoka describes coming ashore in Luneta Park, famous for its beautiful sunsets.

The road, which ran alongside a canal, was lined with large leafy trees whose tops were crimson. I imagined them to be the flame trees mentioned in the lyrics of a popular song. There was a fragrance in the air that might have been the smell of grass wet from the ceaseless rain of the rainy season, or the smell of damp earth. Weary as I was from the long ship ride, these sights and smells filled me with something approaching exultation. I felt that this was one of the happiest moments of my life; I could only be grateful to the fates for granting me such happiness before I died.

My thirty-five years were not always happy, but neither had I ever suffered unbearable misfortune. Now I was doomed to end my life as part of a defeated army in the Philippines—rotten luck to be sure. Yet if, prior to that unavoidable death, I could experience this moment of happiness, maybe it was all right. Without the immediate prospect of death, whether I would now feel so happy was doubtful.[14]

Here again we see a precise awareness concerning the mysterious conditions pertaining to the happiness of the soul. The soldiers had arrived in a death trap from which they knew escape was impossible; they were resigned to imminent extinction. Ōoka Shōhei, as a mature intellectual among them, saw the situation with particular clarity—yet what came over him was a sense that this was the happiest moment of his life. He himself found his reaction surprising. To be killed in a losing battle is decidedly unfortunate, yet astoundingly, he found himself thinking that this prior moment of intense happiness made his coming fate tolerable. Then he arrived at a paradoxical truth: "Without the immediate prospect of death, whether I would now feel so happy was doubtful."

And so Ōoka Shōhei discovered for himself in 1944 the very truth expressed centuries earlier in *Essays in Idleness*.

Now Is the Time to Cast off All Bonds

Yoshida Kenkō advises that to live well, one should as far as possible avoid getting bogged down in daily affairs and live concerned only with essen-

---

14 Ōoka Shōhei, *Hitō ni tsuita hojūhei*, in *Ōoka Shōhei zenshū*, Vol. 2 (Tokyo: Chikuma Shobo, 1994).

tials, with matters of the heart. He expands on this advice by specifying in section 112 just how a person aware that death hovers near ought to live out his or her days.

Which of the common run of social responsibilities are not difficult to avoid? Anyone who submits to all his worldly obligations, feeling that he cannot very well ignore them, finds himself besieged by requests, physically stressed and mentally fraught; in the end, he fritters his life away, ensnared by a tangle of petty obligations.

The day is waning, the way ahead long. My life is stuck. Now is the time to cast off all bonds. I will not keep commitments, nor worry about propriety. Let any who cannot understand how I feel call me mad. Let them think I have lost all reason and humanity. Abuse will not bother me, and I will turn a deaf ear to praise.

To paraphrase, human activities of all kinds are difficult to disentangle yourself from. If you resign yourself to observing ceremonial occasions, proper manners, and all social conventions, afraid of seeming rude, you will be bombarded with requests and experience physical hardship; above all, your mind will never be at ease. Your life, choked by a mass of petty affairs, will come to nothing.

Then what to do? The hour is late and there is still far to go. My life is a mess, bobbling in uncertain circles. Now is the time for me to get rid of all my ties. I won't bother doing things society expects me to do. I know it's considered only proper to do them, but I'm not going to. I'm throwing it all overboard. Anyone who can't understand my feelings can think I've lost my mind; that's fine with me. "You have no grasp of reality; you're heartless"—whatever they may say, I don't care. Criticism will roll off my back, and I won't lend an ear to praise.

In short, Kenkō says the thing to do is throw aside all social conventions, rules, and customs and live for yourself, satisfying the needs of your own heart.

At the age of fifty-five, when I reached retirement, this advice hit me with particular force. As I walked along I would chant to myself, "My life is stuck. Now is the time to cast off all bonds." I actually did give up attending ceremonial and social occasions. Declining to attend funerals has been far from easy, but I have done it, and I have also stayed away from parties of every kind. I have ignored the norms of society and lived just as I pleased; past the age of sixty I think that's what everyone should do. If even in old age we conform to society's every expectation and jump through all its hoops, then just as Kenkō says, we end up spending our lifetime on frivolous matters, stuck in a pointless loop. Nothing could be more inane.

Weddings have long been taken over by commercial interests, but now the same is true of funerals; they are flashy with little meaning, so it feels good not to have to go to them. I would rather mourn the deceased quietly by myself. Such behavior ceases to be problematic, it seems to me, once a person enters old age and no longer belongs to an organization. Failing to offer compliments at every turn in life should not be regarded askance.

During the European Middle Ages, the slogan "*memento mori*" (remember death) was seen everywhere, an injunction to meditate on death. The sense of *memento mori* in *Essays in Idleness* isn't a reminder of life's evanescence—the rosy-cheeked youth of morning turning to white ashes by evening—but a reminder that our lives unfold in the midst of death and that because death is alongside us, ever present, we need to live each day fully aware of life's preciousness and make the most of our time.

Live in Tranquility

And now, the famous section 75:

How could anyone ever weary of a life of idleness? It is a fine thing to be alone with nothing to distract you.

Follow the ways of the world and your heart, captivated by the world's impurities, will be easily led astray; mingle with others and your conversation will adapt to their responses, no longer coming from the heart. You are by turns flippant and quarrelsome, resentful one moment and elated the next, your emotions in constant turmoil. You are overly judgmental and endlessly absorbed in questions of profit and loss. Delusion becomes a form of drunkenness, and with drunkenness comes delirium. Harried and distracted, you neglect to contemplate the things that matter. This is how all human beings are.

Even if you are unacquainted with the true Way, by removing yourself from the company of others and living in tranquility you can remain aloof from the world's affairs and enjoy peace of mind, happy for the time being.

A literal translation of the title of Kenkō's book, *Tsurezuregusa*, would be "Grasses of Idleness." The word *tsurezure*, "idleness," usually implies bored inactivity, but Kenkō gives the condition a positive spin. Here is my paraphrase of his comments.

I fail to understand people who express dislike for idleness. Instead of pandering to the world, how much better to be alone and see things as they are! If you accommodate yourself to the ways of the world and do as expected, your heart, distracted by the impurities of mundane affairs, is easily led astray; and if you place importance on dealings with others, you worry so much about the impression you will make and how the other person will respond that you end up speaking for him or for her and cease to be yourself. By turns teasing, quarrelsome, resentful, or happy, you are never settled. You obsess over rights and wrongs, what is good and what is bad, and focus blindly on your own interests, forever thinking in terms of profit and loss. Not only are you totally deluded, but you live in a state of seeming drunkenness. It's as if in your drunkenness you are dreaming dreams, too engrossed ever to wake up and take a good look at yourself.

The solution, even for those still ignorant of the true Way (Buddhism, as it may be, or any other enlightened way), is to distance yourself from all connections and obligations, including social etiquette, and live not in restlessness but in tranquility. Do not become embroiled in the world's affairs but let your heart be at peace. This above all is how to enjoy, here and now, your life for the time being.

You don't need to know the true Way, says Kenkō—you don't need to have reached Buddhist enlightenment or any other form of supreme wisdom. Just disentangle yourself from all your commitments and connections and live in tranquility: this is his ultimate message. I have taken his words to heart and aim constantly in my life to uphold the ideal of tranquility.

8

If You Are Determined to Achieve One Thing

Live from the Heart

Last time I said that to live in tranquility is Yoshida Kenkō's ideal, and therefore the ideal advocated throughout *Essays in Idleness*. To avoid being caught up in the world's tribulations and maintain serenity of body and mind is the ideal way of life.

What Kenkō despises above all is being made the world's pawn. In our time, this would mean, for example, being worked to death by one's company, boss, or partner; being forever subjected to worry and exhaustion, forever caught up in calculations of profit and loss. Living according to the ways of the world deprives you of freedom and brings only suffering: this way of thinking, which goes hand in hand with the longing for tranquility, permeates *Essays in Idleness*.

For example, in section 134, written in his old age, Kenkō says, "If you know that you have grown old, why not live in tranquility and set yourself at ease?" Toward the end of the book, in section 241, he writes, "When you immediately abandon all and enter on the Way, there is nothing to hinder you and nothing to bind you; mind and body are tranquil." This above all was Kenkō's vision of the ideal life.

Section 60 tells the story of someone who did not allow himself to be dictated to by others but lived as he pleased, master of himself:

In the Shinjō monastery, there was an abbot of great wisdom named Jōshin. He loved sweet potatoes and ate quite a lot of them. Even when delivering a sermon, he kept a big bowl heaped high with sweet potatoes at his side to munch on as he read aloud. If he fell ill, he would retire to his cell for a week or two and heal himself by eating all he wanted of the finest sweet potatoes, consuming them more than ever. In this way he was able to cure every sickness. He never let others share his sweet potatoes, but ate them all by himself. Although he was extremely poor, when his teacher died and left him 200 kan in cash and his hermitage, Jōshin sold the hermitage for 100 kan and set aside the entire sum of 300 kan for the purchase of sweet potatoes. He entrusted the money to someone in Kyoto and drew out 10 kan at a time, in this way keeping himself well supplied. He never spent the money on anything else but used it entirely on sweet potatoes. People marveled, "For a poor man like him to receive 300 kan and spend it this way shows he is a true saint!"

This same abbot saw a certain priest and called him Shirōruri. When people asked what a "shirōruri" was, he replied, "I don't know either. But I can tell you this—if there were such a thing, it would look like him."

Jōshin was good-looking and strong, a man of enormous appetite who excelled in calligraphy, scholarship, and speaking. He was also a leading light of Buddhism, highly regarded by all in the temple; but as an eccentric who thought little of the world, in all things he suited himself and never did another man's bidding. When he officiated at a memorial service and sat down afterward to eat, he didn't wait for everyone to be served but began eating as soon as his tray was brought, and he left as soon as he was done. He didn't eat with others at fixed mealtimes or any other times but ate whenever he felt like it, whether in the middle of the night or at dawn. If sleepy he would retire in the daytime and not come out even if implored to attend to some urgent matter. When he woke up, he would go several nights without sleeping and wander around quietly muttering to himself. Even though he was so unusual, people didn't dislike him but forgave him everything. It must be because he was a man of great virtue.

This is the only place in *Essays in Idleness* where Yoshida Kenkō takes up a single individual and affirms all his actions—but not because he, Kenkō, is capable of acting the same way. Rather, I think he longs to be free and holds up Jōshin as his ideal. To live at the dictates of one's heart, utterly free and not despised by others, and to be an "eccentric who [thinks] little of the world," disdaining the world's ways and living from the heart, are the two things Kenkō envies in Jōshin. In short, Jōshin lived Kenkō's ideal life.

If You Are Determined to Achieve One Thing

I too am incapable of following in Jōshin's footsteps, and yet from around the age of sixty I made a conscious decision to live like him. The lines "My life is stuck. Now is the time to cast off all bonds" became my mantra. I actually do live an untrammeled life now, going to bed at seven and getting up at four or five in the morning. I never attend funerals. I do as I please—the greatest blessing of old age.

In section 188, Kenkō further sets out how we ought to live. This passage forms a pair with the previous one:

A certain person who wanted his son to be a priest advised him, "Study hard and learn the law of cause and effect; make your way in the world by lecturing on the sutras." The son obediently decided to do just that and started off by learning to ride horseback. Having neither palanquin nor ox-cart, he was afraid that when summoned to officiate at a Buddhist service, if they sent a horse for him and he fell off, unable to sit well in the saddle, it would be most distressing. Next, assuming that after the service drinks would be served, he decided the parishioners would think their priest a dull fellow indeed if he had no talent, so he learned to sing ballads. The more he improved at horsemanship and singing, the harder he worked to achieve yet greater mastery, and ended up growing old without ever having found time to learn the sutras.

Not only this priest but all people are prone to act this way. Young people think they will make a name for themselves in various fields and accomplish something grand; setting out to pursue scholarship and polish their abilities, confident that they have a long life ahead of them, they take their time. Soon they are so distracted by daily life that all their plans fall through, and before they know it they are old, having never become proficient at anything or achieved the kind of life they had imagined. Too old to start over, whatever their regrets, they waste away with the speed of a wheel rolling downhill.

If you have things you want to accomplish in life, decide which one is most important to you and devote yourself to it, forgetting the rest. Of the flood of things that come at you during your lifetime, or during any given period of time, choose only those that will help you to reach your goal and forget the rest. Hasten to do one important thing. If you fail to abandon the rest, you will accomplish nothing.

This section sums up what Kenkō wants to say: choose one thing that you truly want to do, and forget everything else. I heartily concur.

Matsuo Bashō, in his work *Knapsack Notebook*, wrote "At last, having no ability or skill, I followed this one course"—the path of *haikai*, the precursor of haiku. As he says, it is not a question of talent or the lack of it; if you really love something, you will pursue it tirelessly and, as can be seen from many real-life examples, ultimately attain first-rate status. Those who try their hand at everything generally don't amount to much.

Further on in section 188, Kenkō makes this comment:

> If you are determined to achieve one thing, don't take it to heart if other things come to nothing, and don't be ashamed of ridicule. Unless you give up all else, you won't achieve the one important thing.

In other words, when you set your sights on a goal, even if you accomplish nothing else, don't worry about it. Even if people jeer and accuse you of knowing nothing, you have no reason to be ashamed. Unless you abandon everything else, you won't accomplish the one goal most important to you. This is an amazing statement, and it's undeniably true. You need to make up your mind that you will accomplish one certain thing. It won't do to make your choice based on what is currently popular or what seems vaguely appealing. Doing so, however talented you may be, would leave you as a jack of all trades and master of none.

In Kenkō's case, the "one thing" he aimed for was Buddhist practice. Dōgen constantly cautioned his disciples in the same way, telling them that the Buddhist practitioner must focus only on his practice and let everything else fall away. It's generally true: whether you want to be a top scholar or a Noh master like Zeami, you must stake your all on your dream. Section 188 mentions a go player, and the same can be said of those who seek to master the game of go. They devote themselves to the game from early childhood, sacrificing everything from school grades to other pastimes to broad knowledge, living only to play go. Such singlemindedness is the path to excellence. I am acquainted with a certain go player who came to Japan from Korea at the age of six and devoted himself exclusively to the game. By the time he was eighteen, he was a past master. Concentrating the great energy of youth on his goal yielded this result.

"If you are determined to achieve one thing, don't take it to heart if other things come to nothing." This advice holds true in all aspects of life.

Kamo no Chōmei

c. 1155–1216

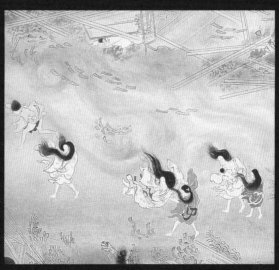

Illustrated Hand-scroll of Tales of the Heike, "The Whirlwind"
(detail), Hayashibara Museum of Art

A poet, critic, and essayist. His religious name was Ren'in. In 1201 ex-emperor Gotoba chose him to work in the Poetry Bureau, but barely three years later, at age 50 he retired from the world. His works include *An Account of My Hut*, *Collection of Religious Awakenings,* and *Nameless Notes.* He was also a renowned player of the *biwa*.

9

A Remarkable Master of Prose

Attachment to This World

An Account of My Hut by Kamo no Chōmei is one of my favorite classical texts—a "desk-side book" of mine, to use an old phrase. Not all of the classics appeal to me. *The Tale of Genji*, for example, has long been held up as the greatest masterpiece of Japanese literature, but it goes against my grain; over my lifetime I have tried and failed several times to read it and other similarly famous works. But *An Account of My Hut* I turn to with pleasure again and again, along with *Treasury of the True Dharma Eye*, *Tales of the Heike*, *Essays in Idleness,* and *Tales of Now and Long Ago*; poetry anthologies such as *Ten Thousand Leaves* and Saigyō's *Mountain Home Collection*; the poems of Bashō and Buson; and *kyōgen,* traditional comic theater.

Chōmei's *An Account of My Hut* and Kenkō's *Essays in Idleness* are often lumped together, but in my opinion they are quite different. Reading the latter, one is constantly aware of the presence of someone with an uncannily cool and observant eye. *An Account of My Hut* suggests rather a man of simple honesty, far removed from the realm of spiritual enlightenment. To the very end Chōmei retains his attachment to this world, unable to set aside his grudges and obsessions or his greedy curiosity, clinging tenaciously to his flawed self. What makes *An Account of My Hut* so appealing is, I believe, the eminently human qualities of its author. Where *Essays in Idleness* suggests the hand of a sage, in *An Account of My Hut* we encounter a man of letters with a modern self-awareness who lived in a manner true to himself. That is extremely refreshing.

Kamo no Chōmei became a monk and a recluse in 1204 at the age of fifty. Saigyō retired from the world at age twenty-three, Kenkō at thirty; compared to them, Saigyō's renunciation of the world came quite late in life. In an age when life expectancy was fifty, he clung to the world as long as he possibly could, until finally he couldn't bear it anymore and became a monk. As I see it, he didn't renounce the world so much as he was ejected from it, laden with unremitting bitterness and regret.

An Account of My Hut contains this deceptively simple declaration: "In the spring of my fiftieth year, I left home and retired from the world." Documentary evidence such as the diary of Chōmei's friend Minamoto no Ienaga, however, indicates that circumstances surrounding his action were far more complicated than these words would suggest.

Retired emperor Gotoba gathered representative poets of the time in the Bureau of Poetry to begin editing the eighth imperial poetry anthology, *New Collection of Waka Ancient and Modern*. Chōmei was one of those selected, and he worked diligently at his task. As a reward, Gotoba decided to make him shrine priest at Kawai Shrine, located on the grounds of the important Shimogamo Shrine. When Chōmei got wind of this appointment, he "shed tears of joy," writes Ienaga. But Kamo no Sukekane, the chief priest at Shimogamo Shrine, soon raised a strongly-worded objection. Since he occupied the most powerful post in the shrine complex, Gotoba was forced to listen. In a change of plans, the ex-emperor elevated a different shrine to the status of imperial shrine and sought to install Chōmei there as the new shrine priest. He bent over backwards to make this unprecedented act of goodwill, confident that it would be welcomed.

However, Chōmei rejected Gotoba's show of kindness. He was so disappointed that his dream of one day succeeding his father as head of Shimo-gamo Shrine had been thwarted that he went into seclusion and no longer even reported to the Bureau of Poetry. The young ex-emperor, twenty-five years Chōmei's junior, was naturally angered by this snub. Ienaga, until then favorably disposed toward Chōmei, writes that his friend was acting out of "sheer stubbornness" and even calls his behavior "mad." In short, hidden behind the serene line "In the spring of my fiftieth year, I left home and retired from the world" lies a messy human drama.

The intransigent stubbornness that led Kamo no Chōmei to rebuff Goto-ba's gesture is characteristic of him. It's just this foolish attachment to self that I like so much about Chōmei and that makes *An Account of My Hut* so appealing.

The Death of Chōmei's Father

Kamo no Chōmei was born in 1155 as the second son of Kamo no Naga-tsugu, the chief priest at Shimogamo Shrine on the Kamo River in Kyoto. Kamo no Sukekane—the one who blocked Chōmei's appointment—was the successor to Chōmei's father. Even today the shrine grounds are impressively huge, occupying hundreds of thousands of square meters, and in the twelfth century the area was forty times greater. The chief priest had extraordinarily large land holdings. Nagatsugu, who owned seventy estates in twenty-three provinces, was a man of vast income, property and influence. At the time of Chōmei's birth, however, his father was only seventeen, and as Chōmei was the second son, Nagatsugu presumably became a father at fourteen or fifteen, which seems awfully young even for those days. In any case, he remained chief priest at Shimogamo Shrine from the time he was seventeen until his death at thirty-four. His acqui-sition of power at such a young age may have given rise to various problems, which might help to explain why his successor, Sukekane, felt such enmity.

Chōmei wrote that when his father died, he became an orphan. That sense of loneliness would determine the course of the rest of his life. He not only grieved at the loss of his father but became embroiled in an unpleasant conflict with his clan in which he came out the loser and was baldly rejected, falling into a wretched state with nowhere to turn. For a man of eighteen, a full-fledged adult, to apply the term "orphan" to himself is rather pathetic and certainly telling: the death of his father clearly shook Chōmei to the core.

An Account of My Hut includes these words: "Since I first became aware of the nature of things, some forty springs and summers have gone by." He wrote the essay at age fifty-eight. In other words, he learned "the nature of things" at eighteen, on the death of his father.

Ienaga writes in his diary:

> On becoming a complete orphan, Chōmei ceased associating with the shrine and confined himself to home. His poetry brought him to court, where, after becoming a fellow of the Bureau of Poetry and submitting poems to the constant poetry competitions, he toiled night and day.

On losing his father, Chōmei left off doing shrine work and devoted himself to poetry at home. In time he began to submit poems to *uta-awase*, poetry competitions that were then highly popular. In the space of four years he participated in sixteen competitions with considerable success. He gradually was recognized as a poet and began to frequent the palace, then was made a contributing editor of the eighth imperial poetry anthology, working on it "night and day." It is easy to imagine Chōmei's excitement as, having won the approval of ex-emperor Gotoba, he found his place in the world.

As Ienaga indicates, Chōmei confined himself to his paternal grand-mother's home after losing his father. It appears that he married someone in that household and fathered a child, but at around age thirty he left his wife and child and took up residence near the Kamo River. Here is how he describes that transition:

> I inherited my paternal grandmother's house and lived there for a long time. Then, lacking connections in the world, I fell on hard times, and although I had many fond memories of the place I could not stay there any longer. In my thirties, I built a house to my liking. It was a tenth the size of my former home.

The interesting expression "Lacking connections in the world, I fell on hard times" shows his literary bent. Unable to succeed to his father's post, he found it difficult to go on living in his grandmother's house, and his declining fortunes finally forced him to leave. He says he went to live in a house only one-tenth the size of his ancestral home, but it would still have been fairly large. He was then named to the Bureau of Poetry and devoted himself to his job there.

A discourse on poetry by Chōmei entitled *Nameless Notes* contains a rather boastful anecdote under the heading "The Cicada Brook Incident." At a poetry contest held at Kamigamo Shrine, Chōmei entered this poem in the category "poems on the moon":

Ishikawa ya	Rock-strewn river—
semi no ogawa no	Cicada Brook
kiyokereba	is so pure and clear
tsuki mo nagare o	the moon has come to dwell
tazunete zo sumu	in its limpid stream.

The entry was disqualified on the grounds that there was no precedent for the phrase *semi no ogawa*, "Cicada Brook." Chōmei afterward demonstrated that it was another name for the Kamo River, and his poem went on to win acclaim. This incident shows how deeply immersed he was in poetry.

I don't find this poem of his all that interesting, however. Later on, after it was selected for inclusion in the new imperial poetry anthology, he wrote, "My joy is great enough to form a lingering attachment in the next life," that is, to be an impediment to enlightenment. But he is quick to add, "How useless!" Happy that his poem has been chosen for such an honor, he then mocks the uselessness of being happy about such a thing. Chōmei always takes a good hard look at himself. Comments such as this are typical of his style, and I find them very appealing.

A Born Journalist

Kamo no Chōmei's strength as a writer lies not in his poetry but in his unbounded curiosity regarding contemporary events and his ability to record his impressions in vivid prose. *An Account of My Hut*, in other words, is where he comes into his own. Despite its brevity, the essay describes a surprisingly large number of events. Not only is his attention highly focused, but he shows tremendous skill in conveying the salient points of each event with precision. It is astonishing that he was able to use the Japanese language of his era to create descriptions of such powerful realism. Though poetry was central in his life, the antennae of his curiosity were always attuned to the currents of the times. When an incident occurred, he quickly verified it with his own eyes, showing great ability to respond, observe, and communicate.

Chōmei begins his essay with an account of the Great Fire that swept Kyoto in 1177, when he was twenty-two, and goes on to describe four more natural disasters, including the moving of the capital by Taira no Kiyomori in 1180 and the famine of 1181. Here is his account of the Great Fire:

> On the twenty-eighth day of the fourth month of 1177, on an unquiet night when a strong wind raged, at eight in the evening [a different contemporary source gives the time of the outbreak as ten P.M.] fire broke out in the southeast part of the capital and spread northwest. Flames engulfed the Suzaku Gate, the Palace Great Audience Hall, the university, and the Ministry of Popular Affairs, turning them to ash in a single night. They say the fire originated in Higuchitomi no Kōji, in a shack housing dancers. Spread by the wind, the flames shifted here and there, spreading out gradually in the shape of an open fan. Houses far off were enveloped in smoke, while those nearby were caught up in flames. The night sky filled with ashes, bright red from the reflected light of the fire, and the conflagration kept shifting as flames leapt 100 to 200 meters at a time, whipped by the wind. People caught in the middle were bewildered. Some fell to the ground, choking on smoke; others were trapped in the flames and died instantly. Still others barely managed to escape alive, but lost all they owned. Untold treasures were reduced to ash.

This passage, which would take up no more than a single sheet of writing paper, is beautifully composed in lean, taut prose that vividly conveys the fierceness of the fire. The description is masterful. The line "an unquiet night when a strong wind raged" sets the tone, foreshadowing some sinister event.

During World War II, American B29 bombers dropped incendiary bombs on Japan's large and medium-sized cities, and the damage far exceeded that from the fire Chōmei brings to our attention. Yet his description—"The night sky filled with ashes, bright red from the reflected light of the fire, and the conflagration kept shifting as flames leapt 100 to 200 meters at a time, whipped by the wind"—applies perfectly. Having witnessed similar scenes in various cities myself, I can well imagine that when Chōmei heard there was a fire, he dashed out of his house and ran around finding out the source of the fire and tracking its progress through the capital.

According to Chōmei, the fire began in housing for dancers, but recent research tells a different story. A farewell party for a samurai being punished by exile to the provinces became drunkenly raucous; somebody cut off his own ear as a goodbye present, and in the end the revelers set fire to the building. That seems to have been the origin.

What gives Chōmei's words such power is the realism of his descriptions, which are based on his observations. The passage, though short, is hard-hitting.

The account of a tornado that ripped through Kyoto when Chōmei was twenty-six is equally riveting.

Again, in the fourth month of 1180, a great whirlwind struck in Naka-no-mikado Kyōgoku and swept as far as Rokujō. Raging through town, it cut a swath 300 to 400 meters wide. Not a single house, large or small, was left standing. Some were flattened outright, while others were left with beams and pillars alone intact. Sometimes a gate would be carried off and set down 400 or 500 meters away; elsewhere a fence would be blown away, uniting adjacent properties. Innumerable household possessions were blown sky-high. Cypress thatching and shingles whirled in the air like winter leaves. Clouds of dust rose up like smoke, blinding the eyes, and the roar of the wind was so fierce that not a word spoken could be heard. The winds of hell could be no worse.

This short description too is written in a tight economical style that vividly recreates the tornado's ferocity. Again, Chōmei is most likely describing scenes that he saw with his own eyes. Witnessing and recording such events seems to have energized him more than anything else. In that sense, he was a born journalist.

Kamo no Chōmei wasn't a thinker like Yoshida Kenkō, nor did he write epics like *Tales of the Heike*. A poet by profession, he joined the Bureau of Poetry at Gotoba's personal invitation, achieving unqualified success in contemporary poetry circles—and yet I would venture to say his poems are not first-rate. They are the fruit of his study of poetry. His natural genius lay rather in writing accounts of events such as fires, tornados, famines, and the moving of the capital. He was a master of journalistic prose.

10

Taking Pleasure in the Absence of Grief

Witness to the Times

Chōmei applied brilliant intuition, curiosity, and powers of observation to real-world phenomena—changing times, human events, power shifts. Nowhere are his gifts on more abundant display than in his accounts of the moving of the capital in 1180 and the great famine of the following year.

The capital was moved to Fukuhara (present-day Kobe) because of a sudden, whimsical decree by Taira no Kiyomori, the most powerful political figure of the day. Chōmei shows how the abruptness of the decision sent panic-stricken people scattering. Here again, he felt compelled to visit Fukuhara to observe firsthand the situation in the new capital. Something came over him and gave him no peace unless he did so.

Much later, at what was then the advanced age of fifty-seven, after he had gone to live in seclusion on Mt. Hino, Chōmei traveled all the way to Kamakura to meet with Shogun Minamoto no Sanetomo. His penchant for action was thus lifelong. The idea of Chōmei as someone whose unquenchable curiosity drove him hither and yon even in old age I find intensely human and winning.

Here is Chōmei's account of what he saw in Fukuhara:

Then I happened to visit the new capital in the province of Tsu and found it too narrow to lay out a proper grid of streets. To the north was a towering range of mountains; to the south, the land sloped into the sea. The roar of the waves was incessant, the salt wind ferocious. The palace in the mountains, suggesting the Round Timber Palace of old, I found surprisingly stylish and elegant. Houses were being torn down and floated downriver every day, so many they clogged the waterway; where could they be getting rebuilt? Much of the new capital is vacant land, with few complete residences. The old capital has been lain waste and the new capital is unfinished. Everyone feels as unsettled as a drifting cloud.

This description also is worthy of savoring by reading aloud. Chōmei tells us he "happened to visit" the new capital, but it is far likelier that he went there on purpose. The Round Timber Palace he refers to was a temporary palace made of timber with the bark left on, constructed in the seventh century in Asakura, on the island of Kyushu, at the time of Empress Saimei's preparations for war against Silla. Chōmei caps his observations with this brilliant summation: "The old capital has been lain waste and the new capital is unfinished." In a single sentence he expresses keen historical awareness. This sentence alone makes me revere *An Account of My Hut.* It could go into any history book and is applicable in various situations. Seldom has anyone so succinctly and neatly summed up a time of transition. This line, a model of historical narrative, deserves high praise.

Yet of the five descriptive passages that provide eye-witness accounts of history, the finest is the one on the famine of 1181. Chōmei must have worn himself out walking around and observing the dreadful scenes he describes.

Then in the Yōwa era, I think it was, although it was so long ago I cannot be sure, there was a terrible famine that lasted two years. In spring and summer there was drought, in autumn and winter gales and floods; conditions were so bad that none of the five grains ripened. In spring the soil was tilled in vain; in summer the seedlings were planted, but in the fall there was no harvest and in winter no bustle of putting food in storage. People everywhere left the land where they lived and crossed borders into new areas, or abandoned their homes to live in the hills. Prayers of all kinds were recited and special rites were carried out, to no effect. The capital normally relies on the countryside for all its supplies, but as nothing was forthcoming, people could not keep up appearances. Hunger drove them to offer up their finest possessions in exchange for food, virtually giving them away, but there were no takers. The occasional person willing to barter held gold cheap and grain dear. Beggars lined the roadsides, their voices raised in a miserable clamor. So ended the first of the two years.

The following year, people hoped the situation would improve, but instead a plague was added to their woes and things were worse than ever. People everywhere were starving, like fish in a pond gasping for air as the water level recedes. In the end, even properly dressed people with hats on their heads and footwear on their feet would go begging from door to door. The poor wretches would be walking along one moment and fall dead to the ground the next. Bodies lay by fences and roadsides in uncountable numbers. With nowhere to dispose of them, the stench filled the world, and as decomposition progressed, the sight was too terrible to look upon. The banks of the river were so strewn with bodies that horses and vehicles could not pass by.

Anyone in Japan who experienced World War II will remember that during the war, even the finest kimonos had little value, and their owners exchanged them for a handful of rice, fighting back tears. The same thing happened in Chōmei's day, as people received little for the treasures they offered. Chōmei also describes in vivid detail the horrors of famine. My older brother died in the battle of Imphal in Burma, so I have read many accounts of what happened there; soldiers didn't die fighting but instead succumbed to starvation and disease. Records indicate that they died exactly as Chōmei describes, tottering along like ghosts one moment, collapsing and expiring the next. The dead were left on the road where they fell, and fierce tropical squalls quickly reduced their remains to bone. The road where they lay became known as "Skeleton Road." The horrors that Chōmei saw were exactly like this. The overpowering smell of death, which he describes as a "stench [that] filled the world," is unimaginable to those who have never experienced it.

This short passage makes clear that Chōmei, while holding his nose at the foul smell, gazed with lively interest at a world in which corpses lay all about with no one to remove them. Though the sight was "too terrible to look upon," he didn't avert his eyes but kept right on looking.

The Difficulty of Life

What drove Chōmei to seek out even such grotesque reality, when he was under no obligation to do so? Most nobles of his day, men like the brilliant poet Fujiwara no Teika, spent their time sitting in their mansions thinking about poetry; they certainly didn't go wandering the streets the way Chōmei did, like a man possessed. It is that state of possession that made *An Account of My Hut* possible and that ensured his fame over the centuries, down to our day.

Chōmei lived in a completely different way from Kyoto courtiers, townspeople, and intellectuals. His poetry conforms to the standards of the day, but he set greatest store by his own spirit and lived as he pleased. That's the sort of man he was. When he was happy, he would make exclamations of joy and gratitude. If something interested him, he would go to any lengths to see it for himself. After writing about famine, earthquake, and so on, he makes this confession:

> When an insignificant person like myself is in the presence of a great personage, although I may feel pleasure there is no great happiness, and even if grieving over something, I cannot raise my voice in distress. My comings and goings are not free; I tremble like a sparrow in the vicinity of a hawk's nest.

He goes on to say that someone like him, a poor man without pull, finds life truly difficult.

> Rely on others, and they own you. Protect others, and your emotions control you. Following the world brings hardship; not following it makes you seem like a madman. Where and how can one find even a moment's peace or rest one's heart even slightly?

Relying on other people gives them ownership over you, and setting great store by others binds the heart with emotional ties. Those who abide by society's conventions feel constrained and cramped: these words express a deep truth. Attempting to live in accord with society's conventions is a source of hardship, says Chōmei, a sentiment found also in *Essays in Idleness*; yet dare to reject society's mores and people will think you have gone insane. Where and how should one live in order to feel secure and know even a fleeting peace of mind? "Following the world brings hardship; not following it makes you seem like a madman." This famous line resonates with truth. In our age, the same lament echoes in the depths of everyone's heart.

From this passage it is easy to deduce that all the while Chōmei was hard at work in the Bureau of Poetry, serving faithfully at the command of the retired emperor Gotoba, he felt constrained and asked himself why he had to endure such suffering. Then when he spurned Gotoba's goodwill, causing even Ienaga, his lone sympathizer, to denounce his "hard heart," he must have truly felt that "not following [the world] makes you seem a madman." His words come straight from the heart. That's what I like about Chōmei.

Taking Pleasure in the Absence of Grief

Eventually, Chōmei turns away from the world and builds himself a minimal dwelling ten feet square, but his life there is not given over single-mindedly to Buddhist devotions. He does as he likes.

> When I tire of saying the *nembutsu* and my reading of scriptures grows lethargic, I rest and am as lazy as I please. No one is there to reproach me or make me feel ashamed. I have not taken a vow of silence, but living alone as I do, my lips are stayed naturally from sins of speech. I need not make any special effort to observe the commandments, for lacking any companion, how should I be tempted to break them?

Normally, people don't reveal their laziness or willfulness. Chōmei, however, being highly self-conscious, is aware of just how half-hearted and noncommittal he is, and he admits it openly, which I find fascinating.

His hut contains a musical instrument, and at such times he plays for his own entertainment. Above all else, "my humble dwelling is peaceful and without fear." In the capital, people perish in fires, tremble in the shadow of those in power, and otherwise have a hard time; Chōmei treasures his time in his hut, where he can be at peace, free of care. What mattered most to him was the state of his own mind. If he could be tranquil and at peace, then he was in paradise.

Ryōkan was the same, and we saw this in the writing of Yoshida Kenkō as well; now Chōmei's declaration that his greatest happiness lies in peace and tranquility of body and mind shows him to be their spiritual kin.

> The osprey lives on crags because it fears human beings. So it is with me. One who understands the nature of things and the transience of life seeks nothing and makes no great exertions. His only hope is tranquility, and his joy is the absence of grief.

Ryōkan and Kenkō would relate to this idea of taking pleasure in the "absence of grief." Rather than seek a positive joy in life, they too relish the lack of worry or apprehension. The Japanese cultural tradition, it would seem, finds supreme delight not in the enjoyment of some activity but rather in the absence of woe and the simple pleasures of a quiet, fulfilling life.

"I built this hut for myself," Chōmei says, "and not for anyone else." His small dwelling is for himself alone, for the sole purpose of living in peace. He describes his state of mind this way: "Since abandoning the world and becoming a hermit, I have had no resentment or fear." Living as a recluse has left him without any lingering bitterness or anxiety. He is content to entrust all to the workings of fate, to commit his life to the hand of providence. This state of mind is exactly what we observed in the poetry of Ryōkan. Neither clinging to life nor weary of it, he is like a drifting cloud, seeking nothing and lacking nothing. His greatest joy is to doze upon his pillow, and his greatest hope is to take in the beauties of the passing seasons.

Chōmei closes his essay with these words: "The three realms depend on mind alone." The three realms are the Buddhist realms of existence among which we transmigrate in the cycle of birth-and-death: the realm of beings of desire, the realm of beings with form, and the realm of beings without form. These are all determined by one's state of mind, which can bring joy, pain, or any other emotion. The three realms—human existence—are determined by mind alone. Chōmei lives in his mountain hut and now and then chants the *nembutsu*. He knows full well his own inadequacies, yet in the end, having cast all aside, he lives without resentment or fear, entrusting his fate to providence, neither clinging to life nor weary of it. For one who struggled to find his way to have arrived finally at a frame of mind that savors this mode of being is extremely precious. This conclusion resonates with Japan's cultural tradition.

Kamo no Chōmei also wrote a book called *Collection of Religious Awakenings* containing the stories of various people who abandoned the world and found salvation. It contains many fascinating accounts, but I will restrict myself here to *An Account of My Hut* and close by celebrating Chōmei's attainment, in his life as a hermit, of a state of mind in which his only hope was tranquility, and his joy was the absence of grief.

Dōgen

1200–1253

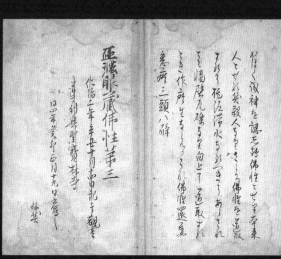

Treasury of the True Dharma Eye, "On Buddha Nature," in Dōgen's own hand, Head Temple Eiheiji

A Zen monk, founder of the Sōtō school of Zen Buddhism in Japan. Earlier in life he also had the Buddhist names Kigen and Buppōbō. He was the son of Koga Michichika, a powerful figure in the imperial court. Dōgen lost his mother at an early age and entered monastic life at age 13, studying Buddhism on Mt. Hiei in Kyoto and at Miidera; later he encountered the Zen master Eisai and studied under him at his temple Kenninji, in Kyoto. In 1223 he traveled to China and after visiting various monasteries studied under Zen master Zhangweng on Mt. Tiantong. He made great spiritual progress and in 1227 returned to Japan to spread the teachings of Sōtō Zen. After a time at Kenninji, he founded the monastery Kōshōji in Fukakusa, on the outskirts of Kyoto, and in 1244 he founded Eiheiji monastery in Echizen (present-day Fukui) and trained many followers. He received the posthumous title Jōyō Daishi. His writings include *Treasury of the True Dharma Eye*, *Universal Recommendation for Zazen*, and *Guidelines for Studying the Way*.

11

On Being

Dōgen's Powerful Use of Language

I am not a Zen practitioner. I have not formally studied Dōgen or done research on him. I am a complete amateur concerning the man I will now be discussing, and yet I have long admired and repeatedly read his work *Treasury of the True Dharma Eye*, which I have always approached with the idea that it can be read not as a Buddhist text but as literature. However, it is awfully dense. I would go so far as to say that of all the books ever written in Japanese, it is probably the most difficult. If you persist in reading it nonetheless, sometimes the clouds part to let through a beam of light, and a phrase or a chapter gleams with sudden radiance.

I am frequently struck and captivated by the incomparable power of Dōgen's writing. Truly there is nothing like it. When I come upon a passage I am able to understand, I recite the words aloud till I know them by heart, and then deep within me I can feel them working on me, saving me. One of the first passages to attract me was the following, from the chapter "Actualizing the Absolute."

> To learn the Buddha Way is to learn the self. To learn the self is to forget the self.

To forget the self is to become one with universal truth. To become one with universal truth is to shed ideas of "my body and mind" and "others' bodies and minds." Enlightenment comes through forgetfulness; once forgotten, enlightenment continues for a very long time.

This is one of the relatively easier passages in the book. As I understand it, he is saying first that to study Buddhism is to learn about or know oneself. Knowing the self means forgetting the self, giving up the attachment to ego. The flow of ideas here is characteristically Dōgenesque.

So what does it mean to forget the self? He says it is "to become one with universal truth." The term here rendered "universal truth" has been variously interpreted. It includes a character that is the Chinese rendering of the Sanskrit word "Dharma," ultimate truth, which contains the literal sense of supporting, upholding from behind. The Dharma is, then, the power which makes us what we are. To let go of oneself and become nothing is to be propped up and saved by that sustaining power.

What does this mean? Dōgen goes on to say that it means shedding all notions of one's own body and mind and those of others. To lose all sense of self and other and become one with the Dharma inherent in all things is to achieve enlightenment. One becomes enlightened, forgetful even of one's enlightenment and so able to maintain that state for a long time. Dōgen warns against attachment even to the state of enlightenment itself.

Parsing the passage in this way isn't interesting in the least, but as I return to the original text time and again, I feel the way of Buddhism penetrating deep into me, and I gain the sense that I understand what it is to learn Buddhism. To try to absorb Buddhist truth through the machinations of the self is wrong. You have to forget the self, shed the self and cast yourself on the Buddha, be saved by the Buddha. That's what it means to "become one with universal truth."

In another, slightly earlier passage, Dōgen writes, "To seek oneness with universal truth while burdened with the self is a delusion. For universal truth to come to one of its own accord is enlightenment." In other words, to attempt to learn the Dharma inherent in all things, that is, Buddhist truth, without casting off the self or the ego—to seek enlightenment that way—is misguided. True enlightenment consists in casting off the self and throwing oneself into the world of the Dharma; the Dharma itself will save you. This passage is crucial in embarking on the way of Buddhism.

Dōgen continues as follows: "Anyone beginning the search for truth is far removed from the realm of truth. When truth is transmitted to the self, a person quickly becomes his true self." "Truth" here means Buddhist truth, the Dharma. When we first seek truth, we tend to think of ourselves as "over here" and truth as somewhere "over there," beyond. We believe ourselves far removed from the locus of truth. But truth is not something with an objective existence beyond ourselves; it lies within us. When we are stripped to nothing, with no ego, no sense of self, having cast away the self, then the Dharma comes and fills our emptiness. When we are emptied and truth fills the vacuum inside us, then we achieve oneness with the universal Dharma.

"When truth is transmitted to the self" means that when truth clearly fills us, we instantly become our true self—that is, a person settled in his or her own truth.

Repeating these words over and over brings a kind of understanding. I have never really known what is meant by the Dharma, but even so, I have slowly come to see that when I cast aside egotism and the self, emptying myself, the Buddha fills and sustains me. And I dimly sense that when that happens, I become my true self.

Severance of Before and After

Dōgen's writing is powerful and vibrant, and despite its difficulty it entrances me. Its difficulty stems from the inherent impossibility of putting Zen concepts into words. The experience of enlightenment cannot be verbalized, yet that is what Dōgen is trying to do. Though Zen awakening is nonverbal by nature, achieved by seated meditation, he is struggling to express it verbally. No one else, apart from D.T. Suzuki in modern times, has ever attempted such a thing. Other Zen masters taught their followers that enlightenment lies beyond the realm of words. Dōgen therefore comes squarely up against the difficulty of trying to express the inexpressible. Therein lies the difficulty of *Treasury of the True Dharma Eye* and also its mysterious power. Eight hundred years after Dōgen wrote his masterpiece, its force hits me directly.

Translations into modern Japanese and commentaries on Dōgen's *Treasury* are legion, and there are any number of sermons on it by Zen monks. I have bought and read several such helps, but in the end, they fail to persuade me. People vary in their understanding of Dōgen. Depending on the translation, the interpretation and commentary can differ widely. I have realized that there is no established way to read the text. Therefore, however difficult a passage may be, however painful the struggle, I read the original words out loud over and over, so often that certain striking passages end up imprinting themselves on my memory. For some fifteen years now I have recited Dōgen to myself while walking, and in the process I have arrived at my own understanding.

And so, although as I said before, where Zen is concerned I am a rank amateur, I would like to describe my experience of reading *Treasury of the True Dharma Eye* as a work of literature. To read Dōgen is in a sense to revolutionize yourself. To grasp what he is saying, you have to change yourself. Unless you have the courage to shed preconceived notions and uproot deeply implanted ways of thinking and judging—your common sense—

Dōgen will remain incomprehensible. The process is both terrifying and wonderful.

As an example, here is another passage from "Actualizing the Absolute":

A stick of firewood, once it is ashes, does not revert to being a stick of firewood. Yet you should not assume that ashes come afterward and firewood beforehand. You should realize that although firewood resides in a dharma-stage possessing a before and an after, the two are cut off from one other. Ashes reside in the dharma-stage of ashes, which has its own before and after. Just as a stick of firewood does not revert to wood once it is ashes, a human being does not come back to life after dying. Buddhists do not speak of life becoming death. They speak of "non-birth." Death does not become life; this is the turning of the Buddha-wheel. This is why they speak of "non-annihilation." Life is a stage in time, and death is a stage in time. It is similar to winter and spring. Buddhists do not consider that winter becomes spring, nor do they say that spring becomes summer.

The first time I read this, I had no idea what Dōgen was getting at, but as I came back to it again and again, slowly it made sense. He starts out by stating that firewood burns and turns to ash, a self-evident fact. He goes on to point out that ashes cannot revert to their former state as firewood, another self-evident fact. Why belabor such mundane matters, we think, and then his next words hit us: "You should not assume that ashes come afterward and firewood beforehand." We are not to view things in terms of before and after or cause and effect: this is the astonishing point of the passage.

Thinking in terms of cause and effect is ingrained in us, but that way of thinking is no good, Dōgen says. Toss out your common sense and all the knowledge you have acquired, become a tabula rasa, and then you will begin to see the truth.

Then what is truth? For firewood, it is the inherent nature of firewood as it is supposed to be. This is the meaning of "firewood resides in a dharma-stage." And for ashes, it is the inherent nature of ashes as they are supposed to be. In either case, there is a before and an after, but the two are cut off from each other. There is complete severance of before and after. The usual temporal concepts of past, present, and future do not apply. All there is is what exists now, this moment. Everything exists in the totality of itself, firewood as firewood, ashes as ashes, and that is all. It is irrelevant and wrong to think in terms of before and after.

This way of thinking was novel to me. Not only does Dōgen completely refute the existence of any causal relationship between firewood and ashes, he also denies the relativity of past, present, and future. Once we rid ourselves of relativistic thinking, there is simply firewood, and there are simply ashes.

Just as firewood, once it turns to ash, can never revert to being wood, a person once dead can never return to life. (His transition to a discussion of life and death takes my breath away.) This is why, he says, Buddhists do not speak of life "becoming" death. They instead speak of "non-birth." Various explanations of the term Dōgen uses here have been offered by translators and commentators, but rather than taking it to mean death as opposed to life, or life as opposed to death, I take it to mean non-birth, being unborn. The passage continues: "Death does not become life; this is the turning of the Buddha-wheel. This is why we speak of 'non-annihilation.'" The teaching that death does not become life is consistent throughout Buddhism. Therefore Buddhists speak of "non-annihilation."

What does this mean? Life is life. The time we are alive is the time we are alive, complete and perfect in itself. Death too is death, complete and perfect in itself. Each of these is perfected in the individual. This is why life and death are each "a stage in time." In the same way, there is winter, and there is spring. We're not to think that winter *becomes* spring. Spring is spring, intact and whole in itself. Summer is summer, perfect and complete. Life is complete in itself.

Having never before encountered this way of thinking, when I first came across Dōgen's idea of the severance of before and after, I felt giddy.

Here and Now

Encountering Dōgen's philosophy of life and death tore to shreds my notions on the subject. I had always thought that Buddhism preached the fragility of human life, impermanence. As the fifteenth-century priest Rennyo wrote, "Rosy cheeks of the morning may become white ashes by evening." But Dōgen is different. He teaches the separateness and completeness of life and death. There is no reason whatever to sense impermanence in that. Since each one is perfect in itself, life and death should be accepted as they are, on their own terms. "Death resides in its own dharma-stage and is cut off from before and after; life resides in its own dharma-stage and is cut off from before and after": the more I murmur the words to myself, the more they seem to represent a truly amazing and revolutionary way of thinking.

The completeness of life as life and death as death is based on the rejection of perceived distinctions such as before and after, cause and effect, and the passage of time. To put it another way, there is only the here and now, where human beings, nature, life, and death are all as they should be. There is no connection of past, present, and future, no cause and effect, no continuation. There is only the eternal Now. What was a thousand years ago, what will be a thousand years hence, and what is now are all contained in this single moment of time; all are alike in the here and now—although to be precise, there is no "now." The void, complete emptiness, is where infinity unfolds. "Here and now" is contiguous with eternity.

This is a stupendous philosophy. I have read these passages over and over and gradually have come to see that everything is complete in the here and now. To carry the idea a step further, even Dōgen, who lived eight centuries ago, is here and now. The moment in time that was Dōgen's "now" coincides with the moment in time that is my "now." Dōgen and I coexist in the same Now. His text taught me this new way of thinking.

A later chapter entitled "On Functioning Fully" contains this statement: "This being so, life is displaying its nature to the full, and death is displaying its nature to the full. You should realize that life and death occur within the immeasurable Dharma embodied in us." To paraphrase, life is life, and all is evident and operational in it. Death is death, and all is evident and operational within it. Therefore, you should know that when we cast these aside and empty ourselves, the Dharma fills us and we attain Buddhahood. In me there is no longer "I," but only the Dharma in all its fullness. I am contained within the Dharma, and life and death occur therein. In that sense, life and death are simply phenomena of the Dharma.

On hearing this, I begin to suspect that death perhaps doesn't amount to much and my life is perhaps fine just as it is. The self is a one-time existence in a specific, particular, historical time, but simultaneously the self exists in the eternal Dharma, beyond space and time, as Life itself. It seems to me Dōgen is saying that to make the most of the eternal Now and live our lives to the utmost is to transcend living and dying.

A little after Dōgen's time, there lived a German Dominican monk named Meister Eckhart. Eckhart had a unique concept of God. In his view, God is not a discrete object of worship but rather exists in the human heart. This way of thinking is strikingly similar to Dōgen's idea that casting the self away and becoming nothing allows the Dharma to fill and sustain the self. One of Eckhart's sermons contains the following passage, which seems to me to echo both Dōgen's idea of the here and now and his concept of eternity:

For just as God is present in the eternal Now, He is present also in this power. If a man's soul were constantly one with God in this power, he would never grow old. That is because the "now" of God's creation of the first human, the "now" of the coming time when the last human shall disappear, and the "now" when I am actually speaking in the present moment are all equal to God, one and the same. Behold a man who abides in the light that is one with God and therefore experiences neither suffering nor the passage of time but dwells in changeless eternity. Truly, such a man is removed from surprise at the unforeseen; all things exist within him in their essential state of being. Therefore, no future phenomena or accidental occurrence ever causes him to encounter something startlingly unexpected and new. That is because he dwells constantly in the sole, unchanging, ceaseless "now." There is undeniable, mystic dignity in that power.[15]

It feels exactly like reading Dōgen. As I wrote before, reading Dōgen amounts to a revolution in thinking. The idea that "before" and "after" are completely cut off from one another is the aspect of that revolution that struck me with the greatest force.

Our flesh is born and, in the course of time, grows, weakens, and dies; all very natural. But we human beings are more than that. We have souls that become one with the Buddha, or God, so that we are present in the eternal Now, beyond annihilation or death. When we attain that state, for the first time we attain true life.

---

15 Ueda Shizuteru, *Meister Eckhart* (Tokyo: Kodansha, 1998). Translated from the Japanese.

12

The Eternal Now

The Living Self

Last time, we learned about Dōgen's concept of the severance of before and after. It follows that human life exists exclusively in the here and now. This is true not only because the past is irretrievably gone and the future has yet to arrive. When we are truly alive, our whole self is in evidence, ever present. We are a true human being. We are, therefore, our absolute self; there is no past or future but only here and now. Perfect fulfillment knows neither time nor space. Precisely speaking, there is neither "here" nor "now," but only the brand-new self and the universe, alive and dynamic. As I see it, Dōgen seeks to convey this truth in his idea of the "severance of before and after."

"Now" is commensurate with eternity. The "One Bright Pearl" chapter in *Treasury of the True Dharma Eye* states that a single instant is equivalent to ten thousand years. Indeed, the "now" of our life is part of eternity and congruent with it. We exist along with eternity. Eternity is not a number; a single instant is eternity. Eternity has nothing to do with numbers. It is absolute.

The self is afloat in an infinity of time with no yesterday or today. When I understood that I was afloat in infinite life, I felt liberated, unshackled.

Often I felt able to sense the oneness of my life with the life of the universe.

I have two dogs, and I walk them early in the morning. When I take them out, the rising sun sheds its golden rays on us. Every time this happens, I feel I have come into contact with something holy, and instinctively I clap my hands in awe. As the sunlight—eternal life—penetrates my being, my self separates from me and is free, one with the universe; my sense that my life, the dogs' lives, and the life of the universe are all one, feels crucially important. The morning sun penetrates me, becomes one with me. The dogs and I and all nature are part of one life. The morning sun is the same as what Dōgen calls the Dharma, and I am embraced by it.

Next let me introduce a moving passage from the chapter "On Functioning Fully." Reading it always gives me courage.

> Life is like riding in a boat. I adjust the sails, handle the rudder. Even when I pole the boat along, it is carrying me; there is no "me" apart from the boat. My presence is what makes the boat a boat. "This very moment" of the boat should be studied with utmost care. In "this very moment," there is nothing apart from the world of the boat. Sky, water, and shore all are of the time of the boat, which is not the same as when there was no boat. Life is what I make it to be, and I am what life makes me to be. While I am in the boat, my body, mind and surroundings are all part of the boat's functioning. The whole vast earth and the whole expanse of space are likewise part of the boat's functioning. I am life, life is me: it comes down to this.

Here Dōgen likens human life to the time when someone is riding in a boat, adjusting the sails and rudder. I, the person in the boat, am causing the boat to move, but the boat is in fact giving me a ride, and I do not exist apart from it. By riding in the boat and moving it along I am making the boat be a boat. Consider that carefully, Dōgen says, and do your utmost to devise ways to ponder and learn from "this very moment," which is a core Zen concept.

When I conceive of the boat as life itself, the metaphor makes perfect sense. We all think we are guiding and controlling ourselves and our life, but we are alive because heaven has provided us with life. My life, the lives of others, the lives of trees and all nature—the life of everything in the universe—all are the same; we all partake of the same life. When we examine the nature of this present moment, we see that everything is part of the world of the boat. The sky and the water and the shore have all become the boat; there is nothing else. This time of the boat is completely different from the time when there was no boat. It's possible to say that my life is what it is because of how I handle it, but by shifting viewpoint, it's equally possible to say that just as the boat bears me up and carries me along, life sustains me and makes me who I am. To ride in the boat means that all of myself—my body and heart, my intellect, and even my environment—is included in the boat's functioning. "The whole vast earth" and "the whole expanse of space" are included as well. "I am life, life is me: it comes down to this."

Let me issue a reminder that renditions of this passage into modern language all differ; I am offering my personal interpretation, presenting the text the way it strikes me. Living is like riding in a boat. I alone trim the sails and rudder and pole the boat to move it along, but in fact the boat is moving me. I cannot be found anywhere but on the boat, which should be thought of as Life with a capital L. My life is a divine gift. That is why I exist. Depending on how I live, my life lives or dies. I adjust the rigging and sails, striving to live well, and my life moves along, but that's not entirely my doing. My life is a gift from the larger Life. Because there is Life, there is me. This crucial point must be well apprehended. Then it is clear that the world is the boat, Life itself. I am Life and Life is me; indeed it is the entire world. Sky and water and shore alike are all of the time of the boat, partaking of Life with me. This is utterly different from the time when I wasn't in the boat, the time before I was born. Because I was born, Dōgen is saying, the world came into being.

The same way of thinking can be found in *The Book of Life-Nourishing Principles*, which the neo-Confucianist Kaibara Ekken wrote in 1713. Human life comes about through the blessing of heaven and earth, our father and mother, so we should nurture ourselves carefully and sustain our lives, the gift of heaven. But Ekken quotes Confucius as saying, "[Responsibility for my] life rests with me, not with heaven." Whether a person's life is sustained for a long time or ends briefly is that person's own doing. This is an ancient teaching associated with the Eastern view of life.

Life exists through me and at the same time shapes me, makes me who I am. This connection is far from easy to understand, but we need to think about it: I feel that Dōgen is issuing us this challenge.

Life is a gift, and we are kept alive from moment to moment. Depending on how the individual lives, his or her life may attain radiant perfection or become shabby and wretched. Perfecting one's life is indeed the purpose of Buddhist practice. Whether we speak in terms of Buddhist truth, or God, or religion in general, this I suspect is a crucial point.

Thinking of life in this way, it does seem to me that the sky, the water, the shore, the boat, and I are all part of the same Life. Dōgen puts it this way: "Sky, water, and shore all are of the time of the boat." They—we—live in the eternal Now. This passage that we read in the previous section I interpret to mean the same thing: "Know that within the immeasurable Dharma there is life and there is death."

Having been given life, I am now alive. I in turn animate the life principle. My existence means that Life is in the boat. Mountain streams, water, the universe—all are "of the time of the boat." When I contemplate these words of Dōgen, my heart is uplifted. I feel tranquil, at peace.

I determine the quality of my own life, make of it what it is. This being so, it follows that those who do not value or attempt to make the most of their lives are wasting something extremely precious. These matters are not only for Buddhist or Zen trainees to ponder. Laymen like ourselves must ponder them as well.

Neither Self nor Other

Dōgen was a master of analogy, and I shall now cite another, similar analogy of his, also from "Actualizing the Absolute."

> A fish in the water, however far it swims, finds the water has no end, and a bird in the air, however far it flies, finds the air has no end. Fish and bird have never, in the past or now, been separated from water or air. They use water or air in great measure when their need is great, in small measure when their need is small. In this way, they make maximum use of their element on every occasion and swim or fly about unhindered wherever they are. A bird that leaves the air will at once die. A fish that leaves the water will at once die. You should know that water is life and air is life. The bird is life, and the fish is life. Life is the bird and life is the fish. This can be taken further: there is Buddhist practice and enlightenment, and human life, long or short. This is the nature of truth.

The passage reads like a parable. It is complete in itself, a beautiful metaphor. A fish in the water can swim and swim without coming to the end of the water. A bird in the air can fly and fly without coming to the end of the sky. But fish and birds are by their nature unable to leave the water or the air. Their movements are great when their need is great, small when their need is small. At all times, they experience the full range of their element; in all places, their experience of their element is total.

But if a bird leaves the sky, it dies. If a fish leaves the water, it dies. Here Dōgen employs tautology, a favorite rhetorical device of his. You must know, he says, that a fish has life because of the water, and a bird has life because of the air. It is equally true that air is life-giving because of the bird and water is life-giving because of the fish. Life *is* the bird, life *is* the fish. Many other conclusions can be drawn. There is enlightenment, and there is the span of human life. Truth, he says, is like this.

By "water" and "air" Dōgen naturally is referring to the actual water and air where fish swim and birds fly in the real world. At the same time, he is speaking of air and water in another dimension—the infinite, boundless world of the Dharma—and of the birds and fish that fly and swim there. That is why however far they travel, there is no end. Fish and birds live in the Dharma; separated from it, they will die.

In the same way, we live in the here and now. Each person lives as a single, ordinary human being. We live and die in the element of time. But if we live in the Dharma, which is water and air, we live to the fullest extent possible. Within the element of time we touch eternity, but separated from it, we die.

This is a truly beautiful passage. We live in the real world, which just as it is becomes the world of the Dharma: this truth is expressed with great beauty. Dōgen continues:

> Now, if a fish or a bird tries to know the extremity of its element before going anywhere in it, the fish or bird will not find its way or its place. Finding your place, finding your way, means actualizing the absolute by following Buddhist practice. The way, the place, is neither large nor small; it is neither self nor other; it is not a holdover from the past, nor has it arisen now. This is the meaning.

If, instead of slipping easily into their element, the fish and bird should first make an exhaustive investigation of the properties of water or air, they would not find a path in either the water or the air. They would have no place there. The same is true of human beings. We live because we are in the Dharma, which we cannot hope to understand by insistent probing with our powers of reason. If you cast yourself into the house of the Buddha—the world of the Dharma—then the Dharma itself will save you. It's wrong, warns Dōgen, to begin by investigating air and water with your intellect before taking the plunge.

Live with this principle firmly in mind, and the path to enlightenment will open before you. Believing that you are already in the vast ocean of life, and undertaking monastic discipline to live that life, leads directly to enlightenment. Then the way to enlightenment becomes clear. "This path" and "this place" are neither great nor small; they cannot be quantified. There is "neither self nor other." Distinctions of great and small, far and near, deep and shallow, before and after, past and present, self and other no longer exist.

In the previous section we came across the line "The body and mind of the self and of others fall away." Falling away refers to enlightenment. To abandon the self is to become emptiness, nothingness, and dwell in enlightenment, a world where there is neither self nor other but all are one and all share the same life. This is a world that has not existed in the past, nor has it only come into existence now. "It all comes down to this": it is as if enlightenment lies before our very eyes.

Unless what Dōgen is saying here is understood with the heart, no words can clarify it. To begin with, abandon rationality. Relinquish functions of the intellect like dualities of right and wrong, good and evil, ugly and beautiful, and enter instead the pre-rational, nondual world. To get into Dōgen's world, instead of trying to understand his words rationally we can only try to experience the ineffable conditions behind them. This probably entails seated meditation or some other form of spiritual discipline, but becoming a Zen trainee isn't for everyone. Dōgen's thinking has to be made accessible to laypeople as well.

In my own way, I try to contemplate a world that can't be expressed through numbers or rationality. Rationality thinks in terms of yesterday, today, and tomorrow, the self and others. Or it distinguishes between beauty and ugliness, life and death, always in dichotomies. The world of rationality continues this process without limit. We can keep on making finer and finer distinctions, but in doing so we will never return to the origin.

In the Western way of thinking, I am here, and outside of me are objects which I use my intellect to rationally comprehend. Dōgen requires us rather to begin by casting aside rationality and returning to the primordial origin that lies, in a manner of speaking, behind us. I call this "the here and now." Zen has many words for it. D.T. Suzuki, the great expositor of Zen in English, calls it "here-now." In other words, the original, single life before any distinction takes place is simultaneously my life and the life of the universe. That primordial state is what we are to return to. That, I think as I read the *Treasury*, is the direction Dōgen indicates, and it is a state of mind that I for one would dearly love to attain.

Laozi, the legendary Chinese founder of Daoism, also promotes not a rational world but a return to primordial life, the true Way. In that sense I almost feel that Zen Buddhist thought merges with Laozi's thinking.

Buddhism spread from India to China, where in place of the speculative, conceptual Buddhism of India, practical Chan Buddhism became the mainstream. I think this course of development made Buddhism easier to understand. And after Dōgen brought this new form of Buddhism back to Japan from China, it went on to become the peculiarly Japanese religion of Zen Buddhism, with teachings that are even more accessible to Japanese people.

In any case, as I walk along saying these words of Dōgen to myself, I feel myself approaching understanding. This is not to say I have reached enlightenment, but I do feel I have attained a degree of clarity. Sensing this brings me joy, and I continue to pore over Dōgen's teachings, totally absorbed. Eight hundred years after he wrote these life lessons down, I love to savor them and feel them quicken within me.

13

Being Is Time

Dōgen's Concept of Time

As I have said, reading Dōgen amounts to a revolution in thinking, and for me, his concept of time in particular has been earth-shaking. We commonly understand time as continuing in a straight line from the distant past into the future, or as something that flows by, never to return. Dōgen's concept is completely different: "Time should not be understood merely as being in flight; we must not learn merely that flight is the property of time."

What is he talking about? We speak of yesterday, today, and tomorrow, based on the common-sense assumption that time proceeds from the past to the future. We divide time into numerical units—a 24-hour day, a 7-day week, a 30-day month, a 12-month year—and live by the calendar. Without these conventions, communal life on this earth would be pretty much impossible for most people, so on one level such a concept of time is a practical necessity.

But besides clock time, we also have subjective time, as when we say "Today was an awfully long day." Since turning seventy, I have been surprised at how much time has speeded up. I find myself saying things like "A year goes by in a flash." In the Tokugawa period, moreover, time was set by the rising and setting of the sun, so a day in summer was up to five hours longer than a day in winter.

Dōgen's view of time is completely different. He is adamant that time does not pass away and that we must not understand it that way. Being is one with the time of here and now. There is no other time, he says.

Earlier I introduced Dōgen's way of thinking about the separation of before and after. Firewood burns and turns to ash. It is a mistake to think that firewood is the cause and ash is the result. The firewood stands alone as firewood and the ashes stand alone as ashes, each having an absolute, independent existence. Firewood has its before and after, but they are separate from one another; firewood exists in its own intrinsic state. Ashes too are complete and absolute as they are. In the same way, Dōgen says, spring is absolute and doesn't *become* summer. Time doesn't flow in an endless stream, yesterday turning to today, then today drawing to a close and so turning to tomorrow. There is only today. Today is absolute. Rather than "today" it would be more accurate to say "here and now." People live always and only in the here and now. The here and now is all there is, and it unfolds without cease. Time is one with our being alive, with the way we live in truth. Being is time and time is being. Dōgen's time isn't something apart from us, like the time we measure with instruments. The period when we are alive, the condition and locus of our being alive—all of that is time.

Therefore our experience—our yesterdays, todays, and tomorrows; our ten years ago and our ten years hence; our youth and our old age—all of it, without exception, is here and now. In that sense we who are alive now are the same as people who lived a millennium ago. We all live in the eternal Now. This is what Dōgen tells us.

Being Is Time, Time Is Being

To Dōgen, time clearly is not the sort of time we are used to, whose passage we measure with clocks. His concept of time is closely connected with being, and with life. His chapter "Time-Being" begins with these words:

> The phrase "time-being" implies that time is the same as existence and all existence is time. Being "a golden figure sixteen feet tall" is time and therefore possesses the sublime radiance of time.

"Being" means existence, so Dōgen is equating time and existence. Everything in existence is time. A "golden figure sixteen feet tall" refers to an image of the Buddha, which, since it exists, is also time. Because it is time, it "therefore possesses the sublime radiance of time." This last is a bit difficult to understand, but Dōgen is referring not to clock time but to independent, living time which, because of its nature, is endowed with the Buddha's sublime radiance. Time and being are one, and my life is part of them; I'm alive in them. Because I'm alive, there is time; my being *is* time. And since my existence is sustained by the Dharma, it partakes of the "sublime radiance of time." Time is thus spiritual. Dōgen must be the first person ever to conceive of the time when one is alive—one's "time-being"—as time contained in the Buddha.

Therefore as long as I exist, time is present and never passes away. For as long as I continue to live, time is always with me. Dōgen calls this *kyōryaku*, an abstruse term commonly glossed along the lines of "traversing"; but I prefer to think of it as "fixed passage" or absolute time, the simultaneous experience of time in its totality.

For example, Dōgen says the following:

> Fixed passage is, for instance, like the springtime. Spring appears in all its variety: this is fixed passage. Consider that spring is not external.

The fixed passage of spring is, perforce, the total experience of spring. Fixed passage is not identical to spring; but the total experience of spring means that fixed passage is fully realized now in the springtime.

In spring flowers bloom, birds sing, gadflies swarm: multiform aspects of spring appear together. Experiencing them simultaneously is "fixed passage." Dōgen tells us, "Consider that spring is not external." In other words, spring isn't something other than myself that I am to experience objectively; rather, in springtime the flowers, the birds, and I all live the spring together: this is Dōgen's fixed passage. When spring is here, when I am experiencing spring, that is an absolute time complete in itself. Experiencing such completion all at once is what is meant by fixed passage. The term does not include the concept of time flying or passing away; rather, the time we experience is incessant, constantly present.

Dōgen further says this:

> Time-being has the virtue of fixed passage. There is fixed passage from what we call today to tomorrow, from today to yesterday, from yesterday to today. Time passes from today to today and from tomorrow to tomorrow. This is because fixed passage is a virtue of time.

To repeat, fixed passage is not a passing away; myself, the flowers, birds, and all live together as one, so I am not bound by time but fly over it with complete freedom. I come from yesterday to today, and I also go from today to yesterday. All time is here and now, and all time is my time. This is the theory of time that Dōgen develops.

When I first read these things I was astonished, but gradually as I got used to them I became able to absorb them naturally. For example, my being alive now means I am alive here and now, and nothing else. The past is gone and the future is not yet here; there is only here and now. Such moments roll forth continuously. That is "time-being." When I die, time ends.

Zen speaks of the absolute present and right now; the point is that here and now connects directly to eternity. Now is included in eternity, and eternity is present in the Now. Dōgen awakens us to the realization that such time is the absolute time of human existence. And so, for example, he also says this:

> My arrayal of myself makes up the entire world. Each thing in this entire world I regard as a moment of time. Things do not hinder one another any more than moments do. Mind is aroused all at once, and that mind gives rise to time. It is just the same with practice and with attaining the Way. The self arranges itself and sees itself. The principle of the self as time is like this.

The basis for the creation of time lies in the self. My existence, my being alive, *is* time. The traces of my being alive, all the "here and now" times and places of my life, are arrayed. That is the entire world; yet though it is the entire world, it's not something external to and apart from me, but something that appears in and through the fact of my being alive. The world I live in, where on one occasion I did this, on another that, and where all those occasions coexist—that is time. Those occasions don't overlap or hinder one another any more than moments of time get in each other's way. The world is the place where I live, and therefore if I aspire to the Way, so does the entire world. The entire world becomes truth within time. The same is true of practicing Buddhism and attaining the Way. All the pathways of my life to this point are interconnected. I look on them, and that is the principle of "self as time," the equation of myself and time. This is a fascinating way of thinking.

The self plays a key role in all this. Temporality and spatiality arise in the wake of my living. Time, space, and I form an inseparable trinity. All are the manifestation of one and the same thing. And Dōgen locates that trinity squarely in the radiance of the Buddha.

I am here, I am there, and I am off in the distance. Just as in springtime flowers bloom, springs of water well up, and gadflies flit about, I am ever present. My acts of arraying all those bits and looking upon them constitute time. Following this line of thinking, Dōgen conceives of time not as something objective and external to human beings, but as something that exists only insofar as we are alive. He also equates time with the awakening of desire to follow the path of the Buddha; his concept of time is increasingly spiritual in nature.

This philosophy of time appeals to me immensely. Normally we live by fitting ourselves to time that is segmented by numbers. Living in society means adapting to society's time, which exists as something apart from ourselves. Whenever this happens we have our existence chopped up as we fit ourselves into an external world order; on each such occasion, we lose ourselves. But if we understand time as our being alive here and now, there is nothing to interfere with us being ourselves. I am entirely alive in this time, and all that is alive is entirely me, and is my time. I am spurred to think that once a day, anyway, I would like to experience this. A way of thinking that is as difficult to fathom as it is fascinating.

Now Contains Past and Future

Past, future, and all time are contained in the present moment. There is no time apart from myself now. This time never existed before and is only of this moment. There is only here and now. Over and over I have told myself these things and have finally grown comfortable with the assertions.

However, Dōgen also says the following: Suppose someone climbs mountains and crosses rivers. After living this way, that person now resides in a magnificent palace. Most people in that situation would say yes, once I climbed mountains and crossed rivers, but now I am here, and all that activity is in the past; I have no connection whatever with those mountains and rivers of long ago. Not so fast, says Dōgen. Since we always live in the here and now, the time when we are alive is all-inclusive. When you climbed the mountains and crossed the rivers, you were there. If you were there, then you own that time, a time that is not vanished but continuously present, connected to the here and now. People assume that time passes and is gone, but it isn't so. The pathways of your life remain in the present, day by day, and nothing is lost.

There's a kind of monster with three heads and eight arms, and I have been that monster, says Dōgen. I have also at times measured 16 feet tall standing and 8 feet seated. I have climbed mountains; I have crossed streams. All of this happened when I was alive, so that time has not passed: it is now, it is my present self.

> Being three-headed and eight-armed was yesterday, being 16 feet tall standing and 8 feet tall sitting is today. Be that as it may, the principle of past-present simply corresponds to the time when I strode into the mountains and the time when I overlooked myriad peaks. Those times have not passed away. My experience of being three-headed and eight-armed is of time-being. Though it seems distant, it is now. I also experience measuring 16 feet tall and 8 feet when seated in time-being, and though it seems distant, it is now.

Difficult as this sounds, he is saying that there is no such thing as yesterday or today. All belongs to the time of "[striding] into the mountains and overlooking myriad peaks." He strode into the reality of mountains and the world and looked out over all the thousands and tens of thousands of peaks at once. That is time. It hasn't passed away. The time of having three heads and eight arms is his time, and so is the time of measuring 16 feet tall standing and 8 feet sitting. It seems remote, but it is all present in the here and now. This is a wonderful statement. The places and times making up the here and now of our life may seem far away and long ago, but they are indeed here and now. We can survey them all in the present. The description of life as a process of plunging into the mountains and looking out on myriad peaks makes sense to me. I've had all sorts of experiences. They haven't passed but are part of my actual experience in life's mountains, and I can now look back on them. They aren't gone. They are here and now. Far off as they may seem, they are part of the eternal present.

This way of thinking lies at the core of Dōgen's view of time, and it is a magnificent concept. Lived experience is time, and time is one's entire lifetime, which connects to eternity just as it is, without one thing lost.

As we have seen, Dōgen also likens human life to riding in a boat. Each of us is the "I" in the boat of life. We make what we can of our life. Life exists through us and, at the same time, we exist because life exists. As we row, all becomes part of the occasion of our life: "Sky, water, and shore all are of the time of the boat." That occasion, when our life appears to us in totality, is the same as when we gaze over myriad peaks. I am in the middle of life itself. That is "not the same as when there was no boat," but now as I gaze over myriad peaks, the peaks are me. I am the mountains.

Elsewhere, in the "Mountains and Water Sutra" chapter, Dōgen says, "The mountains and water here now are the manifestation of the ancient Buddha's path." The "ancient Buddha" is someone who actually lived long ago, and that someone of a past millennium is manifest here and now. I too am manifest with him. We belong to the same time. Time is all existence—literally "time-being"—and it is also Buddhist truth, the Dharma. Such time is not linear, extending from past to future. That linear way of thinking, our common misconception of time, is wrong.

In the year 2000, a worldwide fuss arose about the advent of the third millennium, but I believe measuring the extension of time from the distant past toward the future in such a way leads people astray. "Goodness," we think, "I was born in an insignificant, in-between time, to live for a brief span and then die." From the perspective of eternity, human life is indeed brief and evanescent, as has often been said. But if we focus on our life, everything shifts. The time when we are alive is everything. It encompasses the totality of the universe and all time. It is eternal. That way of thinking offers a way out of our difficulty and, I would suggest, comes close to the actual truth of what it means to be alive.

Reading Dōgen, I've grown accustomed to his sense of time. I've come to feel that the notion of time as extending linearly from the distant past into the future has no meaning for human beings.

The World of the Mind

D. T. Suzuki's "*Ichinen*"

In the previous session we considered Dōgen's philosophy of time, which is completely different from how we ordinarily think of time. The very point I was making is addressed by Zen scholar and Buddhist thinker D. T. Suzuki (1894–1966), who in one of his essays says this about the line *shiki soku ze kū*, "form is emptiness," from the Heart Sutra:

> Emptiness is not absolute quiet and the void, but all things visible and invisible in an undefined chaos, interwoven in infinity; this is indeed the seat of *kū*. Herein lies the meaning of *shiki soku ze kū, kū soku ze shiki*, "Form is emptiness, emptiness is form." ... There is time, and there is space, where diligence is not diligence and endurance is not endurance. Space is time and time is space. They take shape and are perceived in *ichinen*, the present infinite moment. This equivalence is expressed as $0 = \infty$, or "zero equals infinity." This is my own equation.... There is a danger of emptiness being misconstrued as space. Buddhists are always hard put to explain this, as existence is generally thought of in terms of space and not time, when in point of fact space and time are inseparable. It is better to combine them in

the word "*ichinen*" or "here-now." The concept of *ichinen* is of crucial importance in Buddhism. One becomes the Buddha in *ichinen*, which refers also to practice. Shin Buddhism[16] often uses this word "practice," which is not the practice of monastic discipline but *ichinen*, which is itself practice, and it is also referred to as Great Practice, where "great" means absolute. It is not a question of quantity. It is not a state that is obtained by the repetition of the *nembutsu*, "Namu Amida Butsu," but *ichinen* practice itself. Shin Buddhism grew up around this view, which is true faith.

In any case, *kū* is interpreted temporally as "right now." To understand the void, emptiness, is to understand this very moment. The sense of "right now" must be grasped. When it is understood that "right now" is indeed infinite, the equation $0 = \infty$ comes into effect. When we understand that this fleeting moment is infinite in time, we touch the foundation of Eastern thought. [17]

The idea that I have been at pains to convey through the words of Dōgen is here expressed with great simplicity: "space and time are inseparable." They are alive together, and here-now—*ichinen*—is the only time when humans live. Put another way, *ichinen* means "right now," this very moment. When we realize that right now is in fact infinity, then here-now, being neither here nor now, can be expressed as zero. And so zero = infinity. When we grasp that this fleeting moment is indeed infinite, then "we touch the foundation of Eastern thought." This is all exactly what Dōgen has been saying.

---

16 Also known as True Pure Land Buddhism. Based upon the Pure Land sutras and the teachings of Hōnen, Shinran, Rennyo, Ippen and others, it is the most widely practiced form of Buddhism in Japan.

17 Suzuki Daisetsu, "Jiyū kū tadaima" in *Tōyōteki na mikata*, revised edition (Tokyo: Iwanami Bunko, 1997).

There is no other time for us to live than here-now. It is contiguous with infinity. Time and space are inseparable, according to Suzuki, and Dōgen says so too. Dōgen refers to the whole world as "the universe in all ten directions." The entire universe is in fact the self. *Treasury of the True Dharma Eye* contains this statement, for example:

> "In the universe in all ten directions, there is not a single person that is not myself." This being so, each and every person, each and every fist, is the universe, and all are myself. Because all are myself, each self is the ten directions. The ten directions of each self are intimately enmeshed. The life-thread of each and every one is in the palm of my hand, and so each one repays the original cost of his or her straw sandals.

Since the "here and now" when I am alive is the whole world, throughout the universe in all ten directions there is nowhere that isn't me. Each Zen practitioner and each clenched fist, wherever he, she, or it may be, is the universe in all ten directions. They are the ten directions and they are the self. Nobody's world is not the self. Therefore each and every self is the universe in all ten directions.

As long as you keep focused on the fact of your being alive, you are beyond doubt the whole world and the whole world is you. And because all is you—the self—the ten directions of each and every person are intimately interconnected. The life of each and every person is in the palm of your hand. Then existence is not separated into self and other but has returned to its original undivided form.

When you are truly alive, the whole world is your true self. Not only are you the whole world, but the world and its mountains and rivers are all you yourself. All are one. You and the world are not separate. Where I live here and now, the world is. If I hold up my fist, my fist is the entire world, the realm of life. Being alive has nothing to do with small and large, near and far, self and other, host and guest. Where I live and where the Buddha lives is the universe in all ten directions, an infinity of space that cannot be measured numerically, expressed in terms of distance, or grasped through relative notions of perspective or size.

Dōgen's Concept of Space

Dōgen's way of thinking about space is also fascinating. Just as time cannot be measured numerically, neither can space be expressed in relative terms of distance or perspective. One's own true living self is space, just as one's own true living self becomes time. We discussed "fixed passage" previously, and a similar concept applies to space. For example, in the "Ancient Mirror" chapter Dōgen makes this staggering claim:

> If we say the world is ten feet wide, then the world is ten feet wide, and if we say it is one foot wide, then it is one foot wide. Moreover, the "ten feet" we are speaking of and the "one foot" we are speaking of are not some arbitrary measurements.

This passage is elucidating the words of a Tang dynasty monk named Xuefeng, who said this: "When the width of the world is ten feet, the width of the Ancient Mirror is ten feet. When the width of the world is one foot, the width of the Ancient Mirror is one foot." Dōgen wrote this to explain what Xuefeng meant by "ten feet." If a person who has become his true self says "ten feet," then that is the world. The world cannot be measured by distance, time, or any other form of numbers. If I say "ten feet," the world is ten feet wide, and if I say "one foot," the world is one foot wide. The ten feet exist in this very moment, the here-now of my existence. Likewise, "one foot" refers to one foot in this very moment of my existence, not to an objective standard of measurement.

The passage continues as follows:

> In examining the origin of this, people generally think of the world as "immeasurable, boundless thousand-millionfold worlds" or the "inexhaustible world of the Dharma," but this is like our own petty self, pointing beyond the neighboring village. In referring to this world, he says it is ten feet.

Why does Dōgen say these things? It seems that in speaking of the size of the world, people commonly say that it is boundless and immeasurable, that no one knows how far it extends. In truth, numbers—even "thousand-millionfold" and the like—cannot express the world's dimensions. The world is my tiny self, here and now. It's like saying the world is beyond the neighboring village. That's why he says the world is ten feet wide. If one's existence alone is truth, then the world can be ten feet and ten feet can be the world; the world can be one foot and one foot can be the world.

Earlier, we read the passage stating that "I arrange bits of myself and make of them the whole world, and all the separate things of this world I regard as times." We arrange such things and look at them, and our doing so is time. This is similar. The world is not a place where anything is 2 or 3 kilometers away. The world is oneself, oneself is the whole world. The animated place where space and time intersect is what Suzuki calls *kū*, emptiness. To borrow that term, *kū* contains time, space, myself, and the Buddha.

This is all getting harder and harder to follow, but I find Dōgen's world highly enjoyable and feel redeemed by it. Rather than the dualistic Western world where subject and object are separated and all is strictly laid out according to the rules of perspective, this subjective, completely flexible and fundamentally nondual world has come to captivate me.

A World Where All Is Mind

To sum up, just as time in Dōgen's world has nothing to do with calendars and clocks, space to him is not measured by distance but is the manifestation of one's own life, of being alive. This is why ten feet can become the world and one foot can also become the world. If there are mountains and rivers, they become me, and they become the world. I think we may call this the world of the mind. Dōgen also has this to say: "In short, mountains and rivers and the great earth, the sun and moon and stars: these are the mind." Natural phenomena—the great earth with its mountains and rivers, the sky with its sun, moon, and stars—all are in fact manifestations of the mind. They point to the world of the mind; they are concrete indicators of it. When the world appears to us this way, what principle is manifest? Mountains, rivers, water, and the Buddha all belong to the world of the mind: this is a staggering concept.

In the "Time-Being" chapter Dōgen states:

> Mountains are time, and oceans are time. Were there no time, there could be no mountains or oceans. Do not suppose that the present moment of mountains and oceans is not time. The end of time would mean the end of mountains and oceans. If time has no end, then mountains and oceans too have no end. This principle is why the morning star appeared, the Buddha appeared, enlightenment appeared, the udumbara flower[18] appeared. This is time.

---

18 A fragrant flower said to bloom once every 3,000 years, the last time heralding the birth of Buddha.

Now we are really in deep. As I have said repeatedly, Dōgen does not see the time when a person is alive as something measurable or objectifiable. Space and time all become manifest in the reality of being alive. They *are* the reality of being alive. Therefore, when I climb a mountain or cross a river, that entire experience is time.

Mountains are time, and oceans are time. Otherwise they wouldn't exist. The here and now of mountains and oceans mustn't be taken as anything other than time. Being is time. Time is being. That is why a mountain is time and an ocean is time. This living moment of mountains and oceans is none other than time. If time disintegrates, mountains and oceans will too. If time remains intact, mountains and oceans will too. This is an unfailing principle of Buddhism. Therefore, this principle contains the morning star of salvation, and the Buddha, and the way of the Buddha.

All of this is the world of the mind. On we proceed to yet more amazing territory. Whether the mind has become natural phenomena or natural phenomena have become the mind, we can now see that everything in Dōgen's world—nature and the self, human life and death, the universe and the Buddha—all is one animate body.

This is not a world of subject and object, objectively distinguishable. All is alive as one, and therefore inseparable. This truth can only be apprehended by immersing oneself in life. Whether the mind is internal or external, whether it comes or goes, we cannot know. But it manifests itself dynamically. That is why in the chapter entitled "On Learning the Way through Body and Mind," Dōgen makes this further comment:

These things are already mind. Is mind outer or inner? Arriving or departing? At our birth, is one bit added to us? At death, does one particle depart from us? Where can we find life and death and our view of them? Until now they have been simply a moment of the mind, then a second moment of the mind. One moment of the mind is one earth with mountains and rivers; two is a second earth with mountains and rivers. Mountains, rivers, the earth and so on are neither existing nor non-existing, so they are neither great nor small, neither acquirable nor unacquirable, neither knowable nor unknowable.

This is the same as what he has said before, but differently phrased. The sun, moon, and stars are all the mind. Is our mind within or without? Does it come to us or leave us? When we are alive, does it increase by even one little bit? When we die, does even a particle of it leave us? Where can we take our thoughts about life and death? All that has been said here amounts to a moment or two of the mind. The here-now of life is the here-now of living in unified space and time; that moment is the same as all the mountains and rivers of the earth.

Therefore a moment or two of the mind cannot be expressed numerically. Moments of the mind are absolute. They are the earth with all its mountains and rivers. They are not things that exist or don't exist, nor can they be seen as relatively large or small. They are not things that can or cannot be acquired or even known. Such moments are beyond being penetrable or not penetrable, enlightened or unenlightened. They are the mind itself. The mind itself is mountains and rivers and the great earth. Unless we know this, says Dōgen, understanding of true time, true space, true mind, and the whereabouts of the true Buddha will elude us. All these things arise from the mind and return to the mind.

I find all this rather terrifying to contemplate, but Dōgen says that all these phenomena emerge when people seek to live in truth. They cannot be measured in numbers or grasped in terms of near and far, being and nonbeing, or any such relativistic thinking. Enlightenment, then, means realizing this condition of the mind.

The Merit of Ceaseless Practice

Dōgen's concept of time is incomprehensible if we approach it with pre-conceived notions of distinction, discrimination, separation, and measurement. All is one. This is why his chapter "Ceaseless Practice" sets forth the idea that when one person does ceaseless practice—that is, undertakes spiritual discipline to serve the Buddha and to become his or her true self—the entire world benefits. My ceaseless practice brings salvation to practitioners of the past, and their ceaseless practice brings salvation to me now. The Great Way of the Buddha is a continuous, circular path of supreme practice. It is peerless practice that continues from past to future and from present to past, from self to other and from other to self, around and around in a cycle without end. And so it has always been.

Dōgen also says this:

> The merit of this ceaseless practice sustains us and sustains others. The underlying principle is that when we undertake ceaseless practice, merit accrues to the vast universe in all ten directions. Others may be unaware, we ourselves may be unaware, but it is so. Therefore, owing to the ceaseless practice of all the Buddhas and patriarchs, our ceaseless practice has been made clearly manifest, and the Great Way pervades everywhere. Owing to our ceaseless practice, the ceaseless practice of all the Buddhas has been made clearly manifest, and their Great Way pervades everywhere. Owing to our ceaseless practice, the merit of this cycle exists.

"Ceaseless practice" means living a life of Buddhist discipline. The merit of the ceaseless practice of ancient Buddhas (practitioners of old) is evident today in me and in others. The ceaseless practice that I currently do is blessed by the merit of all the ancient Buddhas. At the same time, the ceaseless practice that I do here and now has the same effect, although no one realizes it, perhaps not even I myself. Thanks to the ceaseless practice of practitioners of old, we are now true human beings, and not only that, our own ceaseless practice enables the practitioners of old to be their true selves. If one person does ceaseless practice, it is the same as if everyone does it.

Because of ceaseless practice, there are the sun, the moon, and the stars. Because of ceaseless practice, there are the great earth and the vastness of space. Everything in this world exists due to ceaseless practice. Because others have done ceaseless practice since ancient times, we now exist.

One includes others; one includes all; one is absolute: this way of thinking informs even Dōgen's discussion of ceaseless practice. If we devote ourselves earnestly to living in the present moment of here-now, our "now" saves not only ourselves but others, including people of long ago. Since now encompasses eternity, the practice I now undertake brings salvation to the distant past. At the same time, the practice of people in the distant past brings salvation to me now.

I find this Eastern way of thinking profoundly beautiful.

15

Life and Death

Life Is Life, Death Is Death

One of my favorite passages in *Treasury of the True Dharma Eye* is the short chapter "Life and Death." I have read it many times. As we have seen, much of Dōgen's writing has a cutting severity and harshness to it, but this passage, assumed to be a work of his later years, is different. The language is mellow and soft, with great profundity. I believe this chapter represents the culmination of Dōgen's thought.

Earlier in our examination of Dōgen we considered his view of human life and death, and there are similarities here. I will refer back to our previous discussion periodically as we proceed. To get the most out of this important passage, I copied it out with brush and ink on paper and have read it so many times I know it by heart.

It is wrong to suppose that we go from life to death. Our life is one stage in time; it already has a before and will have an after. Therefore, Buddhism calls it "life beyond birth-and-death." Death is also one stage in time, again with a before and an after. Accordingly, death is called "death beyond birth-and-death." In what we call life, there is nothing but life, and in what we call death there is nothing but death.

Thus when life comes, we should face life, and when death comes, we should face death and serve it. We must not cling to or wish for either one.

We are wrong to think that life shifts into death: this is what we learned at the very first. Life is like the springtime, which exists only as spring and nothing else. Life is simply life. Just as spring is one stage in time, so is our life. Life has a before and an after, but they are cut off from one another. During life, there is only life. During death, there is only death. Therefore life and death are called non-birth and non-annihilation. When we are alive, there is only life, and when we die there is only death. Therefore when life comes we turn toward life, and when death comes we turn toward death with our whole heart. We must neither resent death nor long for life. This is what he is saying.

Consider again the passage about the stick of firewood and the ashes. You will see that his argument there is exactly the same. In reading Dōgen, the first thing that astonished me was his statement that just because firewood turns to ash, we are not to think that the firewood is the cause and ashes are the result. We routinely think in terms of cause and effect; indeed we know no other way to think about things. Dōgen, however, severs that relationship in two. I found his approach startling, but the example of the stick and ashes is clear-cut. We take it for granted that when a stick burns, it turns to ash, with the stick being the cause and the ash, the effect. Dōgen, however, rejects that premise. Firewood is firewood; ashes are ashes. Firewood is complete in and of itself and exists in the world only as firewood; ashes exist only as ashes. Therefore, it is wrong to speak of them in terms of cause and effect or before and after. Firewood is in the stage of being firewood, with its before and after; the before and after exist, though they are completely cut off from one another. The firewood is itself, distinct from the time before, when it was part of a living tree, or the time after, when it will be ashes. The same is true of the ashes. They didn't come into being because firewood burned to ashes; they exist as ashes in their own right. This is how Dōgen thinks. It took me a while to accustom myself to his way of thinking, but now I see what he means.

Why did Dōgen come up with such an example? He wanted to make a clear statement about human life and death. We naturally assume that a human being is born, lives, and then dies, with life the cause and death the effect. But just as with the stick and the ashes, there is no causal relationship. Life is life and death is death. When we are alive, there is only life, and when we are dead, there is only death. This, Dōgen tells us, is the Buddhist approach to living and dying.

The more I think about it, the more persuasive I find this approach. Looked at in this way, death ceases to be something to be feared. When we are alive, there is certainly only life, so there is no need to fret over the prospect of dying. Both life and death, complete in themselves, are included in the Dharma. In the same way, springtime is one stage of time; winter doesn't "become" spring. In the springtime, there is only spring. This is the foundation of Dōgen's thinking. Summer is simply summer. Life is simply life, death simply death. We are not to think that we move from one to the other. Each is its own stage in time with a definite before and after, but they are severed from one another, cut off. In life there is only life, and in death, only death.

Therefore, he says "when life comes, face life, and when death comes, face death and serve it." This statement is refreshing. Once we are born into this world, we should face life and give ourselves to it completely. When death comes, we should likewise turn to death and serve it. We must neither resent death nor cling to life.

This living and dying are the life of the Buddha. If we hate living and dying and want to cast them away, we are throwing away the life of the Buddha. And if we cling to them, this too is throwing away

Buddha's life by limiting ourselves to Buddha's form. When we hate nothing and long for nothing, then for the first time we enter the mind of Buddha.

This idea is similarly refreshing. The reference to Buddha is difficult and can be interpreted in various ways. As far as I understand it, what Dōgen means by the Buddha and the Dharma is neither any actual person nor Śākyamuni, the historical Buddha. Nor is he taking a relativistic approach and suggesting that the Buddha is whatever I, his reader, most value and honor. Rather, I believe that to Dōgen, the Buddha is Life itself. Life is the self, and it is the cosmos. Life itself, which exists yet cannot be seen, is the Buddha. For the Buddha to enter me means I awaken to Life. The ancient Buddhas, according to Dōgen, are the generation upon generation of eminent monks who appeared in India following Śākyamuni. In China too there were multiple generations of eminent monks; they too are the Buddha. I also, through practice, become the Buddha—"the precious life of the Buddha." In other words, living and dying are the heart—the very life—of the Buddha and of Buddhism.

This is why if we despise our condition and seek to cast it aside, we lose the life of the Buddha. Clinging to life or death is no better. "When we hate nothing and long for nothing, then for the first time we enter the mind of the Buddha." When we neither despise death nor cling to life but affirm it, love it, and live with all our might, then, Dōgen says, we have attained the mind of the Buddha.

Throwing in Your All

"Life and Death" then comes to the essential point, in a passage well worth savoring by reading aloud:

But do not measure with the mind and do not speak in words. Simply detach your body and mind and cast them into the house of the Buddha, letting things operate at the Buddha's initiative, and then, when you go where this leads, neither forcing yourself nor straining your mind, you will separate from living and dying and become the Buddha. Who would want to remain stuck in his own mind?

This passage never fails to move me. Seekers of the Buddha-mind may undergo spiritual training, attain enlightenment or awakening, sit in meditation—but Dōgen is not advocating any of these things here. Instead, he says that anyone at all can immediately slip into Buddhahood. To do so, we must not "measure with the mind"—that is, theorize or make intellectual suppositions. Buddhahood cannot be attained by ratiocination, the application of logic and reason. Also he cautions against speaking triflingly "in words." Words are simply names we attach to things for convenience, unrelated to their reality, and yet when we say them we feel as if we have said something substantial. The world of language is its own world, one that, however necessary, cannot reach ultimate truth. Therefore we are not to fool with words. A Buddhist monk delivering a sermon, for example, may cite various passages of scripture with evident appreciation, but even this is wrong.

"Simply detach your body and mind and cast them into the house of the Buddha," Dōgen says. The instruction comes seemingly out of nowhere, and yet it makes a kind of sense to me. It is an injunction to utterly abandon the self. Elsewhere, in "Actualizing the Absolute," he puts it this way: "To push forward and seek to obtain the Dharma is a delusion; the Dharma coming into the self of its own accord is enlightenment." We err in seeking to propel ourselves toward the Dharma in hopes of attaining it; rather, we need to cast off or shed the self. Only when we have completely done so will the Dharma—ultimate truth—come to occupy us fully. That, Dōgen says, is the nature of spiritual awakening.

His advice is plain: "Simply detach your body and mind." Ceasing to be aware of our body or mind, we are to abandon the self and throw it entirely into the house of the Buddha. What "the house of the Buddha" means I can't say for sure, but I have a feeling I know: he is perhaps saying something like "cast yourself into the world of Life."

Let things "operate at the Buddha's initiative," not actively seeking enlightenment through your own efforts but simply emptying yourself to make room for enlightenment. Then "go where this leads," following the Buddha without a shred of doubt, and "without forcing yourself or straining your mind" you will naturally depart the realm of birth-and-death and become the Buddha, transcendent.

I don't understand it, and yet I feel somehow as if I do. The more I say the words over to myself, the more sense they seem to make.

As I have already mentioned, I walk my dogs every morning. When we set out and the morning sun strikes me, I feel the rays shining deep inside me, making me one with them. I imagine the morning sun to be the Buddha. If I have cast all aside and made myself empty, the sun is able to penetrate me, so that the Dharma lives within me. This, I think, must be what Dōgen means by "letting things operate at Buddha's initiative." I actually feel the morning sun enter into me. This approach may be easier to grasp than what we read in "Actualizing the Absolute."

All of us struggle with the realities of living and dying. The thought of death is terrifying. We are saved if we relinquish both our living and our dying to the Buddha. In the words of Ryōkan, "Carefree, I leave it all to fate." If we entrust ourselves entirely to fate, or to the discretion of the Buddha, there is no reason to fear or be anxious. If we enter into the realm of the Buddha and when we are alive only live, when death comes only die, our attachments will fade and we will find salvation.

On reflection, this strikes me as quite close to the message of the Pure Land monks. In Pure Land Buddhism, the believer chants "Namu Amida

Butsu" and entrusts all to Amida Buddha, who made it his mission to save all sentient beings and vowed that if even one person failed to be saved, he, Amida, would not attain Buddhahood. The basic premise of Pure Land Buddhism is that anyone who chants the *nembutsu* and pleads for salvation will receive Amida's gift of salvation.

In the time of those eminent monks, devout followers of Pure Land Buddhism appeared. They were ordinary tradesmen and farmers, members of the laity who attained enlightenment and lived lives of total dedication to Amida Buddha, casting themselves entirely on him and experiencing his salvation in this life. Shinran wrote that he had no idea whether by chanting "Namu Amida Butsu" he would be saved or whether he would land in hell. That sense of leaving all in the hands of Amida is the essence of "Namu Amida Butsu." Though one might fall into hell for doing so, the believer goes on chanting, secure in the knowledge that anyone saying the *nembutsu* will be saved by Amida.

The Japanese saying "step off the tip of a hundred-foot pole" signifies a final, utmost effort requiring a leap of faith. The image is that of a person poised on the tip of a pole who launches himself or herself into empty space. That leap, I think, corresponds to throwing oneself into the house of the Buddha. What I find especially inspiring is the teaching that anyone who practices Buddhism, not only monks, can attain this spiritual level.

In ancient China there was an eminent monk named Mazu Daoyi who studied under a teacher named Nanyue and attained enlightenment. Until he did so, he polished tiles, it is said.

One day Nanyue went to the hut where Mazu was doing his spiritual training. The disciple stood up to receive his master and bowed respectfully.

"What have you been doing with yourself lately?" asked Nanyue.

Mazu replied, "Recently I have been doing nothing but seated meditation."

"What do you aim to accomplish by doing seated meditation?"

"I aim to become a Buddha."

Then Nanyue picked up a roof-tile, brought it over and set it down, and started rubbing it energetically. Mazu observed this and asked what he was doing.

"Polishing a tile."

"What do you aim to accomplish by polishing a tile? It won't do any good."

"I'm going to polish it till it becomes a mirror."

"How can polishing a tile possibly make it into a mirror?"

"Well, how can doing seated meditation possibly make you into a Buddha?"

This is subtlety well suited to a Zen master. It is heresy to set a goal for seated meditation or any other form of Buddhist training. The training itself is already the Buddha. A tile cannot possibly be polished till it becomes a mirror, but even so, we are to rub it vigorously. This is the path to Buddhahood. Maybe the tile won't ever be a mirror. Maybe sitting in meditation won't make you a Buddha, but the act of polishing—sitting in meditation, polishing yourself—is itself the mirror, is itself the Buddha.

Dōgen affirms this in the following words: "The act of polishing a tile to make a mirror resides in the marrow of ancient Buddhas." Polishing a tile until it becomes a mirror is the marrow of Buddhism. Elsewhere, in a chapter on meditation Dōgen says clearly, "Both ancient mirrors and bright mirrors came about by polishing tiles into mirrors." I believe this means the same thing as "Throw yourself into the house of the Buddha and let things operate at the Buddha's initiative." Whether polishing a tile will make of it a gleaming mirror is uncertain, and whether by throwing ourselves into the house of the Buddha we can be saved is equally uncertain. But in an act of supreme faith, we devote ourselves single-mindedly to practice, polishing our tile. Then we separate naturally from birth-and-death.

The passage quoted at the beginning of this section, which seems to promise that any human being can be saved, is one I like very much. I hope that my listeners too will savor the state of "not measuring with the mind."

Saigyō
1118–1190

Illustrated Hand-scroll of Saigyō (detail), Manno Art Museum

A poet who lived during an age of turbulent transition. His lay name was Satō Norikiyo, his religious name En'i. After serving in the elite private guard of Emperor Toba, in 1140 at the age of 23 he abruptly became a Buddhist monk. He spent much of his time on Mt. Kōya and in Ise, also traveling to Shikoku and the northern part of Japan, devoted equally to the Buddha Way and to *waka*. His works include *Mountain Home Collection*, *Things Heard and Noted*, *Supplement to Things Heard and Noted*, and *Mountain Home Collection of the Heart*. The great imperial poetry anthology *New Collection of Waka Ancient and Modern*, compiled after his death, contains 94 poems by him, more than by any other poet.

16

The Self and the Heart

Poems of the Heart

The older I get, the better I like Saigyō. I keep his *Mountain Home Collection* at my bedside and read several poems before bed every night and again on rising every morning.

In 1946, when I was twenty-one, a collection of essays by critic Kobayashi Hideo entitled *On Impermanence* came out. This was just after the war, so the book was printed on poor-quality paper, a slim volume of just 104 pages consisting of short discussions of Japanese classics. One essay was about Saigyō, and that's where I first learned about the poet. Then for a long time I didn't read him, but as I grew older, his poems began to resonate with me. Many of them are concerned with the heart, for he put himself into his poetry—worries, frustrations, doubts and all. The act of living is integral to his poetry, which is why over the centuries his works have remained fresh.

Saigyō lived during a turbulent age of transition that saw the collapse of imperial government, the ruin of the powerful Heike family, and the establishment of the Kamakura shogunate. It was also a time when *waka*, classical poetry, flourished as never before, resulting in the age of the great imperial poetry anthology *New Collection of Waka Ancient and Modern*.

Court poets were unstinting in their pursuit of beauty. Saigyō, while revered by his contemporaries, worked alone, far removed from imperial poetry circles. While those at court delved into the aesthetics of *yūgen* (mystery and depth) and other poetic ideals, all that mattered to Saigyō was his own heart. All his life he studied the ways of the human heart, that incomprehensible thing. This, I believe, is why his poems are still cherished and never grow old.

Here is a poem Saigyō wrote shortly after becoming a monk, with the headnote "Written on Mt. Suzuka, on my way to Ise after fleeing the world":

Suzukayama	On Mt. Suzuka,
ukiyo o yoso ni	having left the world behind
furisutete	never to return
ika ni nariyuku	I wonder what may lie ahead,
waga mi naruramu	what may become of me?

The poet has turned his back on the world and its cares and is on his way to Ise. He happens to cross Mt. Suzuka and pauses to wonder: what lies in store for his heart, for himself? He feels anxiety for the future, but at the same time, having cast the world off, he is eager to explore the way ahead. The poem expresses this mingling of apprehension and hope.

In the world of Japanese poetry, this query—"What may become of me?"—belongs uniquely to Saigyō at this point in time. There were many other poets in Japan, but none of them looked inquiringly into his own heart the way Saigyō did or thought to ask such a question.

The word here rendered "me" is *mi*, a distinctive word that refers to the whole person without the division into body and heart/mind that is typical in the West. *Mi* is a body-heart composite greater than the ego, a social or even cosmic approach to the self. It is a word that Saigyō loved.

The Heart Drifts Away

Why Saigyō decided to become a monk isn't clear. Experts offer various explanations, but I think it's most accurate to say we just don't know. As I said in the section on Ryōkan, there are various possible motives for leaving the world. In Saigyō's case, it's variously said that he woke up one morning to find a close friend he'd spent the previous day with lying dead, leading to thoughts of impermanence; or that the love he bore someone came to nothing; or that he'd had Buddhist inclinations to begin with. Renouncing the world isn't a matter of any one individual cause, I should think. Weariness with life's messiness turns to an abhorrence that leads to sudden flight. That's how it was with Ryōkan. Saigyō's decision probably grew out of his distaste for the bothersome relationships and tangled politics he was caught up in.

Saigyō was born Satō Norikiyo, the son of a warrior family that held a hereditary post in the imperial guard, which was one of six agencies charged with duties like protecting the palace and escorting the emperor on excursions. The Satō family was an old line originating in the Fujiwara clan's Northern House, which was founded by Fujiwara no Fusasaki, whose grandfather Fujiwara no Kamatari founded the entire Fujiwara clan. In 1135, at eighteen, Saigyō was made a captain of the imperial guard by a system called *jōkō*, whereby official ranks were bestowed on those who made donations of land or money to the court. Simply put, appointments were bought. Such scheming was rampant in court society, and Saigyō must have found the environment oppressive and disturbing.

Some people have an innately religious or metaphysical or literary bent that disposes them to weary of life's mercenary strife. I myself turned to literature in my youth as an escape and have devoted myself to literary pursuits ever since, so I can't help imagining that I have some understanding of the feelings of men like Saigyō. Repelled by discord, they acted on their repugnance and cast the world off. The moment they did so, they no longer had a place in society. They had no status, no possessions, nothing. All they had was their own empty self, the embodiment of *mu*, nothingness. Having become nothing, along with unparalleled freedom they experienced anxiety. Saigyō gives vent to those feelings in the words: "I wonder what may lie ahead, what may become of me?"

This focus appears often in Saigyō's poetry. Here is another example:

ukareizuru	My heart, I find,
kokoro wa mi ni mo	wanders off in ecstasy
kanawaneba	quite out of myself;
ika nari totemo	I neither know where this may lead
ika ni ka wa semu	nor what to do about it.

In this contorted, involved poem Saigyō is engaged in dialogue with himself. The phrase *ukareizuru kokoro*, literally "the heart that is carried away," appears over and over in Saigyō's poems, a sign of his passionate nature. He must have had the repeated experience of becoming so lost in admiration of cherry blossoms, or the moon, or a lover, that his heart detached itself from him and traveled to the object of his affection. He experienced his spirit actually slipping from him, drifting off in ecstasy. That's the sort of man he was born to be, a man whose heart could be literally carried away. Here he is powerless to exercise control. The final two lines indicate that he doesn't know what might become of him as a result of this tendency; whatever happens, happens. He is addressing his own heart, discovering its true nature, I think, as he writes.

Abandoning the world has left Saigyō defenseless, with a heart that floats off to cherry blossoms or the moon or whatever else captures his fancy. At the same time, another self is coolly observing this phenomenon. He has attained self-consciousness, I think we can say, and there is nothing simple about it. While other poets of his day wrote about beauty itself, using aesthetic terms like *yūgen*, Saigyō dealt always with metaphysical or religious feelings and his own troublesome dilemma of possessing a heart that could be carried away.

Seeing Blossoms, Seeing the Heart

Even in his poems about cherry blossoms, Saigyō's heart goes astray. No one has written as many poems about cherry blossoms as he did. I have read them many times and like them very much. Surely no one has ever loved cherry blossoms, especially those of Yoshino, south of the ancient capital of Nara, quite as much as Saigyō did.

Yoshinoyama	Since the day I saw
kozue no hana o	cherry blossoms in treetops
mishi hi yori	on Mt. Yoshino,
kokoro wa mi ni mo	my heart is no longer
sowazu nariniki	here inside me.

The poet went again to Mt. Yoshino to see the panorama of cherry blossoms and found the sight of blossoming treetops so beautiful that his spirit was stolen away; his heart separated from him and ever since has wandered in the sky.

In the minds of Japanese people, Saigyō is indelibly linked to Mt. Yoshino. One time I went there, taking along a book of his poems, and drank in the cherry blossoms. They truly are beautiful. Along with the pale pink of the blossoms, new leaves of deep red slowly unfurl, adding depth to the color. The trees on the mountainsides are mostly cedars, and the effect of masses of pinkish blossoms and deep red leaves against a backdrop of deep green is stunning. I wasn't transported like Saigyō, and yet reading his poems in that setting I felt I could understand why his heart would not stay put.

Elsewhere he also makes this reflection:

akugaruru	My heart
kokoro wa sate mo	so filled with longing—
yamazakura	later on
chirinamu ato ya	after the blossoms scatter
mi ni kaeru beki	will it come back to me?

As long as the cherry trees are in blossom, his heart leaves his body and wanders off. He was born this way and can't change how he is. He can only wonder whether, after the blossoms have scattered, his heart will ever return to him.

Poems such as these show that what matters most to Saigyō is not the cherry blossoms per se but his ability to gauge through them the state of his heart: its yearning for blossoms, its way of becoming so entranced that it separates from him. For Saigyō, blossom-viewing is a window on his inner self. His cherry-blossom poems are not primarily about the beauty of the blossoms. His poems generally are revelatory of his heart—his true self—and this is what keeps them fresh and alive.

Let me give one more example:

kokoro kara	My heart's yearning
kokoro ni mono o	comes from deep within
omowasete	my heart;
mi o kurushimuru	the one tormenting me
waga mi narikeri	is only me myself.

This poem offers another unique conception. Even though the poet's heart belongs to him, it is drawn of its own accord to the moon, blossoms, and the like, and fills with yearning quite beyond his control. The "me" observing his heart inflicts physical and mental torment on him; but since that "me" is none other than himself, he is helpless to do anything about it. Why is his heart the way it is? He ponders the heart that is the source of his suffering and realizes that it is he himself who fills it with yearning; that is how his heart—he himself—is made.

This poem was originally included in a grouping of 110 love poems, but it needn't be read as such. Poet and scholar Yasuda Ayao points out that of the 1,643 poems in *Mountain Home Collection*, 313, or nearly one in five, concern the heart.[19] This shows what an important theme the heart was for Saigyō, and it is what makes me feel close to him. Early modern literature deals straight with questions like these: Who am I? What is my heart? What does it mean to be alive? Having read European, chiefly German, literature from the time I was a young man, I learned to probe the heart or self, so to me these poems of Saigyō's are familiar and hit home. Those by his renowned contemporaries I find lacking by comparison.

Here, for example, is a celebrated *waka* by the acknowledged master, Fujiwara no Teika:

haru no yo no	The floating bridge
yume no ukihashi	of a spring night's dream
todaeshite	has come to an end;
mine ni wakaruru	in the sky, trailing clouds
yokogumo no sora	are parted by a mountain peak.

It's not that I find it opaque. The words "spring night's dream" are in themselves beautiful and suggestive of the delicate love between Kaoru and

---

19 Yasuda Ayao, *Saigyō* (Tokyo: Yayoi Shobo, 1973).

Ukifune in the "Floating Bridge" chapter of *The Tale of Genji.* The phrase "floating bridge" seems natural and beautiful, and I understand that it conveys a dream of tender love. The expression "comes to an end" also makes sense to me. Just as the floating bridge of a dream of a spring night ends, the clouds around the mountain peak come apart and drift away in the spring sky. The clouds are symbols, in other words, of Teika's dream as he contemplates the nature of love. The poem is drenched in captivating beauty, a marvel of poetic craft; and yet perhaps because I lack this sort of imagination, it doesn't move me. In comparison, Saigyō's poems have a direct appeal. It's strange if you think about it.

Saigyō lived during a time of unprecedented flourishing for *waka*, as we have noted, among a pantheon of poets who vied in their mastery of the art: Teika as well as his father, Shunzei, and other Fujiwara men including Ietaka, Yoshitsune, Ariie, and Masatsune. There were also outstanding women poets such as Princess Shikishi, Kunaikyō, and Toshinari's daughter. And yet of them all, the only one still widely read is Saigyō, who held himself apart from the rest. His special place in people's hearts is attested to by a medieval poetic biography entitled *Tales of Saigyō.* Something in Saigyō strikes deep within the sensibilities of Japanese people. I believe it is because he took the proper path of literature.

Leaving the World, Yet Unable to Leave

I mentioned before that I read from *Mountain Home Collection* every night before bed. Some of the poems are quite easy to understand, while others are tangled and confusing. Gradually I came to see that this is because Saigyō did not set out to write technically polished *waka* but rather examined his own heart and attempted to accurately express its state. While the poetry circles of his time were ruled by conventions and taboos against the use of certain words and ideas, Saigyō wasn't bound by such restrictions. He freely used ordinary words and colloquial expressions that others avoided. Using the same word twice in a row was frowned upon, but Saigyō thought nothing of writing *aware aware* (pitiful! pitiful!). He even used hackneyed expressions. Unconcerned with the world's conception of beauty, he kept his eyes trained on his heart and used whatever words were at hand to accurately portray its state; this was his sole concern.

iza kokoro	Come away, my heart!
hana o tazunu to	I'm going to search for blossoms,
iinashite	I will say,
Yoshino no oku e	then be off to Yoshino
fukaku irinamu	to enter mountain depths.

The expression *iza kokoro* (Come away, my heart!) reflects an uncommon way of thinking. Just to be sure, I checked an encyclopedic compilation of *waka* from early times to modern, and *iza kokoro* is not listed. Here Saigyō looks straight at his heart and calls out to it. After the caesura at the end of the first line, the poem continues without a break, the structure giving it a peculiar power. One wonders if any of Saigyō's contemporaries ever used a bold first-line caesura like this. This poem shows that even in terms of structure he did as he pleased, unafraid of solecism.

Here the poet enters mountain depths to refine his heart, away from others; clearly the discipline of solitude was important to Saigyō. Once on a visit to Yoshino I too went deep into the mountains, all the way to the place where Saigyō's hut is said to have been. As I looked out across the valley to distant peaks, I saw white magnolias in bloom amid the surrounding greenery. It struck me as a most pleasant place to live, and I could well imagine Saigyō settling there. His summons to his heart to "come away" is the same as the appeals I make to my own heart.

In his mountain hut, Saigyō composed the following poem.

yo o idete	The joy I feel
tani ni sumikeru	on leaving the world behind
ureshisa wa	to live in this valley—
furusu ni nokoru	the song of the nightingale
uguisu no koe	secure within its nest.

Having cast off the world, he lives in a valley where no one comes. Far removed from life's hurly-burly, his heart is purified. To what can he liken his newfound purity and joy? Just as he is wondering this, he hears the peaceful song of a nightingale in its nest. Yes, that is exactly how he feels. The gentleness of Saigyō's heart comes through very naturally in this poem.

It would be easy to point to any number of similar poems by Saigyō. Some would say that casting off the world means cutting ties to family and other encumbrances to focus on Buddhist practice, but to him it means focusing exclusively on the self, entering into the world of his own heart. His heart is in nature's direct presence, and he watches it come face to face with nature, simultaneously participant and observer.

In becoming a monk, Saigyō chose a world of non-possession, while others sought possessions; a world of anonymity, while others sought fame and wealth; a world of quietude, while others went to busy places; a world of perfect freedom, while others were bound by convention. Drawn to principles antithetical to those of society, along with extraordinary freedom he experienced extraordinary loneliness. That conjunction is the nexus of his poetry.

In one poem Saigyō describes his inability to cast off the world despite having become a monk:

yo no naka o	I've cast off the world,
sutete suteenu	yet it seems I cannot
kokochi shite	do so after all
miyako hanarenu	for I am quite unable
wagami nari keri	to bid the capital adieu.

Even after renouncing the world, he retains a lingering attachment to it, or senses his inability to turn his back on worldly things, for to his chagrin he finds himself loitering around the capital. This poem stands in striking contrast to the one about the "song of the nightingale secure within its nest." Saigyō's poetry gives equal expression to these contrasting forms of self-awareness or consciousness. In this sense, his works portray an interior world of the psyche that genuinely belongs to modern literature. I believe he has much in common with Ryōkan.

17

Rovings

Seeing the Buddha in Blossoms and the Moon

I have introduced a number of poems in which Saigyō laments the way his heart, drawn out of him by blossoms or the moon, goes floating off on its own. The following poem, thought to have been written shortly after he became a monk, is found only in a variant edition of *Mountain Home Collection* under the headnote "Composed with five others who set out their thoughts."

> *satemo araji*   Whatever happens,
> *ima miyo kokoro*   watch now, my heart!
> *omoitorite*   This I have resolved:
> *waga mi wa mi ka to*   unsure if I am what I am,
> *ware mo ukaremu*   from now on I shall roam!

This convoluted poem too requires several readings to work out the meaning, but it is evident that the poet's heart is strongly moved. Here is a paraphrase: "Come what may, watch, heart, for I shall not remain as I am. Though this self is mine, it is not yet wholly mine; I am not free. Having made up my mind that this is the case, I've resolved to go wandering, so

heart, let us be off!" This poem conveys the sense that the poet's heart is a
living thing apart from him, a state that causes him grief.

Elsewhere we find this poem:

kage saete	Shedding clear light,
makoto ni tsuki no	the radiance
akaki ni wa	of the moon—
kokoro mo sora ni	my heart wanders off
ukarete zo sumu	to live in the sky.

On a night when the moon shines bright and everything is clearly visible,
his heart is so drawn to the moon that it leaves him and goes off to live in
the sky. His heart is as clear and shining as the moon. The world of this
poem is again typical of Saigyō. No one else wrote *waka* like this. The sky
referred to is the visible sky, but the same character can also mean "emptiness," as in the Buddhist expression *shiki soku ze kū*, "form is emptiness."
The association seems deliberate.

When in his poems Saigyō is looking at cherry blossoms, they are at once
substantial, blossoms in the real world of phenomena, and transcendent,
blossoms of Buddhist emptiness. This is in line with Dōgen's thinking. As
we saw in the previous section, the mountains, rivers, grasses and trees that
Dōgen sees are real, but also they belong to the void, partaking of the eternal
forms of such phenomena. I believe the same can be said of Saigyō's blossoms and moon. He sees the blossoms in front of him, but at the same time
he sees beyond them to the flower of the Buddha, the moon of the Buddha.

Here is another evocative poem:

saranu dani	Even without this
ukarete mono o	my heart leaves my body,
omou mi no	lost in longing—

kokoro o sasou	how it beckons to my heart,
aki no yo no tsuki	the moon this autumn night!

His heart is always ready to leave him and go wandering, but tonight the moon of the autumn night shines with particular luster, as if trying to lure his heart. The poem depicts a heart that enters the moon and becomes one with it, the union of the two creating a unique world.

In a discussion with Myōe, a monk fifty-five years his junior, Saigyō revealed the essence of his poems: each time he composed a *waka*, he said he felt that he was carving a statue of the Buddha, and that he always composed poetry in that spirit. One truly gets that sense.

Here is a sampling of other poems in this spiritual vein. They're not poems that I specially chose to prove a point, by the way; all Saigyō's works are like this. The first one bears the headnote "As I was coming to a decision about leaving secular life, I and a number of others composed verses in Higashiyama about what we each felt about the spring haze":

sora ni naru	Becoming the sky,
kokoro wa haru no	my heart is now
kasumi nite	as light as spring haze,
yo ni araji to mo	having made the choice
omoitatsu ka na	to leave this world behind.

His heart is the sky. It floats above the earth with the weightlessness of spring haze. He decides to be done with the messiness of society. Various explanations are given for Saigyō's decision to renounce the world, as we have noted, but it seems to me that poems such as this probably come the closest to expressing his true intent, and we should take him at his word.

In the next poem, the world of Buddhist truth and the world of the moon have truly become one.

tomo sureba	My heart,
tsuki sumu sora ni	longing for the clarity of
akugaruru	the moon in the sky,
kokoro no hate o	wanders off and to what end
shiru yoshi mo ga na	I have no way of knowing.

When he sees the moon, his heart flies out of him in longing for its pure clarity. What will become of his heart as it wanders in space? Will it leave him permanently for the sky? There is no way to know. This poem is in the love section of the anthology, but there's no need to restrict its meaning to thoughts of love. I see it as another of his transcendental poems. This is who Saigyō is. Weary of the messiness of life in this world, he turns with yearning in the opposite direction, toward moon or blossoms, through which he sees the world of Buddhism inherent in this world; and yet in the end he is unable to leave the messiness of this world after all.

Here is another example:

yukue naku	I gaze in rapture
tsuki ni kokoro no	at the moon, my heart
sumisumite	crystal clear—
hate wa ika ni ka	what its end may be
naramu to suramu	I can but wonder.

As he gazes up at the marvelous moon, entranced, his heart floats off, destination unknown. Like the crystalline moonlight, it too is serene and transparent. It's as if his heart has become the void Buddhism speaks of. What will become of it?

The First Journey to Michinoku

Saigyō is known as a "wandering poet" because his heart was drawn not only to blossoms and the moon but to travel. In fact, he lived in relatively few places—the vicinity of Kyoto, Mt. Kōya, Ise—and wasn't always perambulating, but I feel that in essence he was a traveler. The reason is again his heart: he never stayed long in one place but always felt compelled to move on to refresh his heart.

Among his travels, the journeys to Michinoku, or northeastern Mutsu Province (present-day Tohoku), loom large. He went there a second time toward the end of his life, when he was sixty-nine. His first journey, undertaken as a young man, stirred and exhilarated him, and it inspired many poems. Essentially Saigyō wrote *Gelegenheitsgedichte*, occasional or improvisational poems. He composed poems as a traveler on the road of life, giving voice to his heart along the way. His works were composed on the spot, unlike those of Shunzei, for example, who would toil deep into the night in his study with a robe thrown over his shoulders, revising endlessly. Some of Saigyō's poems may lack polish, but their very roughness is engaging.

Let's look at some of the poems he composed on his journey to the deep north. Not driven by a mission, he was able to take his time. One thing it's said he wanted to do along the way was explore *utamakura*, places with poetical associations. I'm sure he also wanted to make his own discoveries. The trip is thought to have lasted as long as two or three years. At Shirakawa he wrote the following poem, with the headnote "On a pilgrimage to Michinoku, I stopped at the old Shirakawa gatehouse, where the character of the place added charm and pathos to the moon. I wondered when it was that Nōin wrote 'autumn winds are blowing.' Full of feeling for the past, I fastened this poem to a post":

> *Shirakawa no*　　　At Shirakawa
> *sekiya o tsuki no*　　filtering into

> *moru kage wa*   the old gatehouse
> *hito no kokoro o*   moonlight beams arrest
> *tomuru narikeri*   the human heart.

The monk Nōin, who lived some 130 years before Saigyō, was a renowned poet and a contemporary of the powerful Fujiwara no Michinaga and his son Yorimichi. His most famous poem is this: "Though I left the capital accompanied by spring haze, autumn winds are blowing now at Shirakawa Barrier." Legend has it that he actually wrote the poem somewhere in the capital, tanned by the summer sun, but in any case Saigyō was drawn to Nōin and went to Michinoku in part to follow in his footsteps. When he stayed at the old checkpoint, something in the atmosphere made the moon more beautiful and moving than ever, and he recalled his predecessor's poem. Moonlight filtering through gaps in the ruined roof captured his heart. Saigyō wrote a number of tranquil poems such as this.

Another of my favorite poems in *Mountain Home Collection* dates from this same time. It bears this headnote: "When I arrived in Hiraizumi on the twelfth day of the tenth month, snow was falling and there was a fierce storm. The weather was unusually wild. Having long wanted to see Koromo River, I went to have a look. When I came to the riverbank, the sight of the castle was so marvelous that I was awestruck. The edges of the river were frozen, the scene breathtaking."

> *toriwakite*   In bitter cold
> *kokoro mo shimite*   my heart freezes into
> *sae zo wataru*   bright clarity
> *Koromokawa mi ni*   at Koromo River where
> *kitaru kyō shimo*   I have come this very day.

The headnote indicates the date was "the twelfth day of the tenth month," which corresponds to midwinter. I mentioned before that Saigyō's travels in Michinoku stirred and exhilarated him, and this one especially gives that impression. Saigyō—or Satō Norikiyo, his samurai identity— was related by blood to Fujiwara no Hidehira, ruler of Mutsu Province and protector of Minamoto no Yoshitsune. Saigyō was a young man when he composed this poem, and it suggests an awakening of his samurai spirit. The poem is not merely about the bitter cold and austerity of winter; the scene before him has become one with his heart, deeply stirring the spirit of Satō Norikiyo within him.

At first I assumed that this was one of Saigyō's later poems. If it were written in 1185, this would be exactly the time when Minamoto Yoshitsune was on the run, pursued by his brother Yoritomo, eventual founder of the Kamakura shogunate. The house of Fujiwara in Mutsu was also then in danger. This, I assumed, was why Saigyō was especially moved by what he saw. Even now I cannot quite rid myself of that notion. However, experts agree that this poem was written during his youth, without any connection to Yoshitsune's betrayal and death or to the fall of the Hiraizumi Fujiwara. And yet it almost seems as if he has a premonition of what is to come, of the fate that lies in store for Mutsu. Of all his poems dealing with *uta-makura*, including the tranquil poem on the Shirakawa gatehouse, this one stands out. It is a superb piece of poetry.

The poet's spirit is transported. And as he looks upon the castle on Koromo River amid the swirling snow, his heart, frozen in the cold, achieves bright clarity. As usual in Saigyō's poems, the poet is looking not only at what is before him, the castle in the snow. The focus is on himself as he looks at the river under attack by a blizzard. His heart is frozen and attains bright clarity, and this has happened only here and now. Of all his poems, I believe this may be his finest.

Cherry Blossom Poems

As I mentioned before, Saigyō's poems are *Gelegenheitsgedichte*, occasional and improvisational in nature. In the course of his life and his journeying, he examines himself and writes about his heart. This makes his poems very different from works that are rewritten painstakingly in the confines of someone's study. They may be rough, angular, and hard to understand at times, but all of them clearly portray Saigyō the man and the state of his inner being. That makes them inexpressibly delightful to me.

Mountain Home Collection is divided into sections labeled "Spring," "Summer," "Autumn," "Winter," "Love," and "Miscellaneous." Of these, the final section is the most interesting, I think. It consists of question-and-answer poems, reminiscences, travel poems, and *daishirazu*, poems with "no topic." Saigyō once observed that "the poems of the *Collection of Poems from Ancient and Modern Times* should be read as a textbook; the miscellaneous section, especially, should be looked at constantly." He himself writes about his experiences traveling, making those descriptions into headnotes for his poems, which therefore provide a useful guide to how he lived.

And now we must return to the poems on Yoshino and the cherry blossoms there. Saigyō's name is strongly associated with cherry blossoms, not merely because he composed so many poems on the topic but because each one shows the depth of his regard for the blossoms and an astonishing capacity to be transported by their beauty.

Why did Saigyō love cherry blossoms so much, I wonder? It strikes me as mysterious. The poet Ueda Miyoji wrote, "Saigyō's body would float a little above the ground—half an inch or so—in pursuit of his wandering heart. When by so doing he achieved harmony and oneness of body and spirit, he must have experienced this world as an earthly paradise."[20] This seems to me a reasonable and beautiful assumption.

---

20 Ueda Miyoji, *Kono yo kono sei: Saigyō, Ryōkan, Myōe, Dōgen* (Tokyo: Shinchosha, 1984).

But when I read the spring section of *Mountain Home Collection*, what awes me is the depth of Saigyō's regard for the blossoms and the strangely compelling intensity of his emotions. Rather than trying to interpret these things, it seems more important to me simply to savor them.

> *Yoshinoyama*   On Mt. Yoshino
> *sakura ga eda ni*   snowflakes scatter
> *yuki chirite*   on cherry branches—
> *hana osoge naru*   this is one of those years
> *toshi ni mo naru ka na* when the blossoms will be late.

This is the most heartfelt of all Saigyō's poems on the blossoms, a dulcet masterpiece. I think it is truly wonderful. The cherry trees at Yoshino are ancient, their gnarled trunks dark with moss; snowflakes land gently on them, turning them white. The buds have begun to swell, but it is too soon for the blossoms to appear. Ah, this year's blossoms will be late. The extent of the poet's eagerness as he awaits the blossoms comes fully through, and the conclusion has a calm solidity and depth. The poem ends not with the usual grouping of seven syllables but two groupings of four (*toshi ni mo/ naru ka na*), which in this case works well to support the rest of the poem. The best thing to do with a poem like this is sit back and appreciate it, absorb it without rationalization.

Such poems clearly reveal the gentleness and tenderness of Saigyō's heart and his straightforward empathy with nature. Sensing those things is pleasant, but we cannot forget that Saigyō also had tremendous strength of mind. He possessed two complementary sides. His gentle, vulnerable side shows up best in his poems on cherry blossoms.

18

Cherry Blossoms

Waka as a Means of Spiritual Discipline

As I have pointed out, Saigyō was markedly individual and stands out among his peers. No one else wrote about the self, taking the pursuit of self-knowledge as theme and tracing the peregrinations of the heart. "Know thyself" has been the starting-point of philosophies of all kinds going back to ancient Greece, as well as the starting-point of religion, and Saigyō's *waka* can be seen as a means of approaching Buddhist truth. He was trained in the Shingon school of Buddhism, where knowledge of one's own mind is deemed the highest form of wisdom and a means of knowing the mind of the Buddha. This is the direction in which his poetry leads.

At seventy, Saigyō gave the fifteen-year-old monk Myōe instruction in poetry, according to a biography of Myōe by his disciple Kikai. In general Saigyō left almost no writings on poetics, apart from truisms such as "*waka* should be beautiful," but his reported comments here are fairly substantial.

Saigyō frequently came and talked about poetry. His own approach, he said, was far from the ordinary: "Cherry blossoms, the cuckoo, the moon, snow—though the varied forms of nature give me delight, I am ever aware that phenomena of this world are insubstantial. And are not all words that bring forth poetry true words? When I write of blossoms I do not think of blossoms; when I write of the moon I do not think of the moon. I simply delight in them as the occasion presents itself and compose my poems. A rainbow lends color to emptiness; sunlight makes emptiness bright; yet emptiness itself takes on neither color nor brightness. With a heart of emptiness, I give color to the various scenes before me, but leave no trace. My poems are the true form of the Buddha, and therefore composing a poem is the same as carving a statue of the Buddha. Conceiving a poem is the same as reciting the esoteric true words of Buddhism. Through my poems I can understand the Dharma. To carelessly pursue the way of poetry, failing to reach this point, is error."

Clearly to Saigyō, composing poetry is a form of spiritual discipline. He composes poems keeping in mind the Buddhist principle that "form is emptiness." All of nature, the blossoms, the cuckoo, the moon, and the snow, are at once "form" and "emptiness." The words of his poems are one with the teachings of Buddhism, the "true words" of Shingon. His poems on blossoms are not really about the blossoms, and his poems on the moon are not really about the moon. When he sees blossoms or the moon, he simply delights in them and takes the occasion to compose a poem. His poems are the colors of the rainbow and the brightness of sunshine in an empty sky. With a heart as empty as the sky, he delights in the blossoms and the moon as they come before him, but afterward nothing remains. Each poem is the form of the Buddha. Each time he composes one he is carving a statue of the Buddha, and the words that go through his mind are the equivalent of the mysterious "true words" of the Shingon tradition. Poetry takes him into the Dharma, ultimate meaning. Composing poetry indiscriminately without reaching this point is wrong.

Hell-Screen Poems

The collection *Things Heard and Noted* contains poems not included in *Mountain Home Collection*, among them the famous series "On Having Seen a Hell Screen." Saigyō was shaken by a painted screen depicting the torments of hell and wrote a number of poems in reaction.

miru mo ushi	Depressing to see—
ika ni ka subeki	what shall I do with my heart?
waga kokoro	Have I committed
kakaru mukui no	sins this awful,
tsumi ya arikeru	deserving such recompense?

The painting of hell is disheartening and painful to look at. If a mere painting brings on this amount of suffering, what is he to do with his heart from now on? Has he committed sins that would merit his falling into hell and experiencing such torment? The question "What shall I do with my heart?" is Saigyō's recurring refrain. Wherever he goes, he is constantly confronting his inner self and questioning what to do with his heart.

aware aware	Pitiful pitiful!
kakaru ukime o	After looking and looking
miru miru wa	at such appalling sights
nani to te dare mo	people go about their ways
yo ni magiru ramu	as if nothing were the matter!

Here, after marveling at the inexpressible pitifulness of the sights of hell, the poet asks how people can act unconcerned in this life even while knowing what fate awaits them. Why don't they give any thought to the life to come?

The poem contains two repetitions: *aware aware* ("pitiful pitiful") and *miru miru* ("looking and looking"). Saigyō piles on these colloquial expressions without concern. Such repetitions were frowned on at the time, as we have mentioned, but since Saigyō's chief concern is the expression of his heart, he is willing to use any means at hand. Concerning diction he is completely free and nonchalant.

Surviving hell scrolls from the twelfth century portray various horrible scenes; the sight of such paintings left Saigyō severely disturbed. In all he wrote twenty-seven *waka* under this heading, where ordinarily such a series of poems would have been unthinkable. Poets of the imperial court would never have taken up such a topic, which by aesthetic standards of the day was unfit for poetry. By happening to be moved by his experience and composing a series of poems in response, Saigyō again shows himself to be a poet of a different order from his peers. For him, a hell screen is a means of inquiring into the state of his soul. These remarkable poems show the vitality of his sensitivity and imagination.

The Entranced Heart

Saigyō's heart is entranced by cherry blossoms and the moon, moved by a painting of hell. When he looks on physical objects such as these, he sees their form in the void, but he knows that form and void are one and the same and that what he sees is indeed a manifestation of this eternal principle of Buddhism. A poem about cherry blossoms may be beautiful, but to Saigyō it expresses the Buddha.

hana mireba	Seeing cherry blossoms,
sono iware to wa	for no reason
nakeredomo	whatsoever
kokoro no uchi zo	deep in my heart
kurushikarikeru	I feel anguish.

Despite his love for the cherry blossoms, for some reason when he sees them his heart fills with anguish. The thought of their inevitable scattering is painful. The above poem indicates how deeply affecting he finds the sight of cherry blossoms.

Let's look at a few more in the same vein:

hana ni somu	Why should
kokoro no ika de	love of blossoms linger
nokorikemu	in my heart?
sutehateteki to	Here I thought that I had left
omou waga mi ni	everything behind…

Love of cherry blossoms is deeply engrained in him, but why do the blossoms retain this fascination for him when he has renounced the world? Even though he has become a monk, he is helpless to do anything about his passion for the blossoms.

kaze sasou	Enticed by breezes,
hana no yukue wa	the blossoms drift toward
shiranedomo	some unknown end
oshimu kokoro wa	while deep within me
mi ni tomarikeri	my grieving heart remains.

Once they have scattered at the invitation of the wind, where do the cherry blossoms go? He doesn't know. His heart mourning their loss does not go away with them, but stays inside him forever.

All of these poems deal with cherry blossoms, but it is clear, I think, that in each one Saigyō is being introspective and self-reflective.

yo no naka o	When I think

omoeba nabete	of this world,
chiru hana no	all is scattering blossoms;
waga mi o sate mo	What then shall I do
izuchi ka mo semu	with myself?

Everything in this world is as fleeting as the cherry blossoms, including me, but what can I do about myself? He is soliloquizing over the world's and his own impermanence. Toward the end of his life, Saigyō took several poems to show Shunzei and his son Teika, asking their opinion. To his pleasure, Teika heaped praise on the ending of this poem. The line is hardly elegant, but it is characteristic of Saigyō and effectively conveys the sense that his existence weighs heavily on him.

When I read these poems of Saigyō's on the cherry blossoms that so deeply entranced him, I am struck by the richness, gentleness, and mellowness of his poetic sensitivity, expressed in a completely natural style. He loves the blossoms to the point of distraction; his heart is both stirred by their beauty and drawn to Buddhist truth. This attraction is the fountainhead of Saigyō's art and of his poetry. If he were drawn only to Buddhism, he would not be nearly so appealing to us. His poems are beautiful because of his fascination with cherry blossoms and the moon.

Saigyō the Man

Even after becoming a monk, Saigyō went about Yoshino composing poems on the blossoms, the moon, and other aspects of nature. Not everyone found this behavior respectable, as shown in the following interesting account from *Notes of a Frog at the Bottom of a Well*, a pedagogical work by the fourteenth-century monk Tonna containing a collection of anecdotes, lore, and advice on poetry. Mongaku, a warrior turned monk, was famous for his ferocity.

Master Mongaku despised Saigyō. The reason, he said, was that anyone who had renounced the world should devote himself to spiritual practice and nothing else. Saigyō was a disgrace to monkhood for running around acting refined and composing poems. If he ever ran into him, he often said, he'd break his skull. His disciples worried what would happen if their master ever actually did such a thing to the great poet.

One day Saigyō attended a lotus service at a temple in Takao, and went around admiring the flowers. Mongaku's disciples were determined not to let their master know about this. After the service they went back to their living quarters, but before long someone came into the garden and called out.

"Who is it?" said Mongaku.

"My name is Saigyō. I came for the lotus service, but it's getting late and I wondered if I might stay the night here."

Mongaku was more than ready for this encounter. Thinking his chance had finally come, he opened the sliding door and waited. When Saigyō came along, he took a long look at him and then ushered him cordially inside with a respectful greeting: "Do come in. I have long heard about you and wished to meet you. I am delighted that you have come to visit." He showed Saigyō great hospitality, serving him dinner and also breakfast in the morning before seeing him off.

Mongaku's disciples had been agitated with worry, and they were relieved when the visit ended without incident. They asked their master about it. "You always said you'd break his skull if you ever saw him, but instead you and he chatted peaceably. Didn't you go back on your word?"

"You idiots!" Mongaku scolded. "Was that the face of someone I could possibly beat up? It was the face of someone who could beat *me* to a pulp!"

173

I am fond of this anecdote and often tell it. For one thing, it lets us know that Saigyō had a tough-looking appearance. He was a samurai to begin with, so that seems reasonable. Representations of other famous people of the era, including even Shinran, founder of True Pure Land Buddhism, inevitably show them with fierce expressions. Surviving the rigors of the age no doubt called for toughness. Mongaku the "ferocious monk" must of course have been imposing, yet Saigyō had an even stronger presence than he. Not only that, Mongaku must have discussed Buddhism with his guest and realized he was out of his depth. The anecdote shows his recognition of Saigyō's superiority.

Later on Saigyō composed this verse:

Takaodera	Lotus service
aware narikeru	at the temple in Takao—
tsutome kana	charming indeed
yasuraibana to	with shouts of *yasuraibana*
tsuzumi utsu nari	and beating on hand drums.

In other words, the service in Takao was a tasteful event, with people chanting *"yasuraibana"* ("evil-averting blossoms") and beating on hand drums to pray for good health. This poem is also rather fine.

Saigyō's heart may have been extremely natural, gentle, and mellow, but the body encasing it was impressively built, as this episode shows. By always reading quiet poems of Saigyō's and imagining him as a quiet soul, we may lose sight of who he really was.

Let Me Die in Spring under Cherry Blossoms

morotomo ni	Blossoms,
ware o mo gushite	when you scatter,

chirine hana	take me with you too!
ukiyo o itou	My heart is oh so weary
kokoro aru mi zo	of this cruel world.

The poet pleads with the cherry blossoms to take him along when the time comes for them to scatter. He too is weary of this world and would like to flee it; he and the blossoms are one.

ukiyo ni wa	Determined not to let them
todome okaji to	linger in this cruel world,
harukaze no	the spring wind
chirasu wa hana o	scatters blossoms just because
oshimu narikeri	it holds them dear.

Why does the spring wind ruthlessly scatter all the cherry blossoms? Because it holds them dear and doesn't want them to remain in this awful world. The purity of the cherry blossoms is contrasted with the polluted nature of this world. Saigyō may have been thinking of the blossoms as an earthly manifestation of the Pure Land.

The following highly celebrated poem is most likely the expression of a wish Saigyō had held from the time he was a young man.

negawaku wa	Let me die in spring
hana no shita ni te	under cherry blossoms
haru shinan	and let it be
sono kisaragi no	at the full moon
mochitsuki no koro	in the Kisaragi month.

Since he has loved the cherry blossoms all his life, the poet wishes to die under a cherry tree in bloom, in the month of Kisaragi (the second lunar month; March by today's calendar). Saigyō spent his last years in Hirokawa Temple and died there. His death came on the sixteenth day of the second month, exactly as he had wished. Poets of the day—Shunzei, Teika, Fujiwara Yoshinari and Jien—all revered the manner of his death and celebrated it in poems. Their encomiums are interesting. Their respect for the timing of Saigyō's death has an elegance associated with that era that I admire.

First, a poem by the court priest Jien:

kimi shiru ya	After dying
sono kisaragi to	in the Kisaragi month
iiokite	as he said he would
koto wa nioeru	his life in the next world
hito no ato no yo	must be a thing of beauty.

Later Ryōkan visited Saigyō's grave bearing flowers and composed this poem:

taori koshi	Though the flowers
hana no iroka wa	that I picked
usuku to mo	may give off little scent
awaremitamae	do look with favor
kokoro bakari wa	on this heart of mine.

Ryōkan's sincere respect for the earlier poet comes through strongly. He seems to have learned a great deal from Saigyō's poetry, as many of his poems show.

And here is one of my favorite Saigyō poems:

uraura to	Nodding
shinanzuru na to	off to sleep

omoitokeba	I ask myself
kokoro no yagate	if this is this how I'll die—
sa zo to kotauru	my heart answers yes.

As he drops quietly off to sleep, the poet muses that death must be like this, and his heart tells him he is right. The headnote for this poem is "impermanence," and the clear-eyed, calm acceptance of death shown here may account for the quietness of Saigyō's passing.

19

A Born Poet

Literary Tradition

I am so fond of Saigyō's poetry that once I start introducing his poems, it's hard for me to stop. I will continue doing so now, but not because I have any brand-new interpretations to offer. Comments by literary specialists, who are obliged to offer perspectives differing from those of their peers and predecessors, are necessarily abstruse; scholars of Japanese and Chinese poetry alike devote themselves to teasing out meaning and investigating the origin and history of phrases while all too often failing to offer straightforward appreciation of the poem itself. Those of us who love literature do a better job of that, I like to congratulate myself. That is why here I'm not offering anything novel but seeking just to savor the poems.

yami harete	Darkness dispelled,
kokoro no sora ni	in the sky of my heart
sumu tsuki wa	dwells the moon
nishi no yamabe ya	moving ever closer to
chikakunaru ramu	the western mountains' rim.

The topic for this poem is "introspection." In Buddhism, contemplating the heart or mind is a form of spiritual discipline. Just as you might contemplate a flower, or the sky, or the Buddha, you contemplate your own heart until it rises before you. Here the first line indicates that troubles weighing on the poet's heart have vanished, and in his mind of darkness the moon has risen. At the same time, this may also be the moon in the actual sky. As he looks at the moon, it sinks in the west. Since the Pure Land of Utmost Bliss is also in the west, he is saying that his heart is on a path leading to the Pure Land. The second line refers both to the movement of the actual moon toward the mountain rim and to the movement of his heart toward paradise.

yama no ha ni	Watching the moon
kakururu tsuki o	disappear behind
nagamureba	the mountain edge
ware mo kokoro no	my heart too
nishi ni iru kana	travels into the west.

This poem comes with an explanatory headnote: "Looking at the moon and thinking of the west." As the poet watches, the moon drifts across the sky and disappears behind the edge of a mountain. Along with it, his heart enters into the western Pure Land. Such spiritual longing is a common theme of Saigyō's poetry.

The following poem, another favorite of mine, is imbued with the spirit of what became known as *suki*, aesthetic reclusion.

tou hito mo	No longer hoping
omoitaetaru	for visitors
yamazato no	to my mountain home—
sabishisa nakuba	were it not for solitude,
sumiukaramashi	how dismal life would be!

The poet lives deep in the mountains, somewhere so remote and isolated that no one comes to see him anymore. His life there is spectacularly lonely; yet paradoxically, solitude is what keeps his mountain life from being miserable and makes it worthwhile. This poem expresses what it means both to cast off the secular world and to attain a mind of singularly refined taste.

Later poets did not fail to pick up on this vital element in Saigyō's poetry. Matsuo Bashō, who came five hundred years after Saigyō, particularly venerated him and absorbed much of his spirit in elevating the previously slighted *haikai* poetic form to the realm of literature. As one who regarded Saigyō as his teacher and learned from him, Bashō included a note in his 1691 *Saga Diary* about the crux of this poem, zeroing in on it and learning from it.

> The twenty-second day
> It rained in the morning. No visitors again today. I feel lonely and amuse myself by jotting things down. Here are the words: "He who mourns makes sadness his master, he who drinks makes pleasure his master." Saigyō, in writing "Were it not for solitude, how dismal life would be!" made solitude his master.

Another famous *waka* by Saigyō builds on the idea of solitude as a means of deepening sensitivity.

sabishisa ni	If only there were
taetaru hito no	someone else enduring
mata mo are na	loneliness
iori narabemu	side by side we'd have our huts
fuyu no yamazato	in this winter mountain valley.

Someone whose heart has withstood loneliness is likely to understand the way of refined elegance as well as the Way of Buddhism. If only there were someone else like that, thinks the poet. If there were, he would love for the two of them to spend the winter in adjacent huts in this mountain valley.

Buson, the eighteenth-century haiku poet, was not very fond of Saigyō, but he looked up to Bashō. Under the headnote "On a fine evening with no one to visit and no visitors," he composed this haiku:

nakanaka ni   And yet because
hitori areba zo   I'm all alone the moon
tsuki o tomo   is now my friend

He too extols the value of solitude; it is precisely because he is alone that he has become close friends with the moon. It gives me pleasure to trace the flow of the ideal of *suki*, uniting ascetic and aesthetic modes down the centuries, from Saigyō to Bashō to Buson.

Becoming familiar with such classical literary connections nurtures the heart. Buson prized the spirit of unworldliness, of living apart from worldly defilement in a retreat devoted to artistic accomplishment and the desire for Buddhahood. That ideal passed from Saigyō to Bashō to him, expanding through transmission yet remaining fundamentally the same. Later generations can read Saigyō's *waka* and the haiku of Bashō and Buson, and by learning and reflecting on them cultivate their own hearts. By such literary pleasures culture is transmitted; a shared awareness is woven into the fabric of a nation's spiritual or mental life, something that binds people together. Without that process, culture is diminished and lost, along with aesthetic and spiritual ideals. I submit that the harshness of our age is due to the failure to pass on our literary traditions. This tradition that shaped the thinking and feeling of past generations of Japanese from the time of Saigyō to that of Bashō and Buson must continue to be handed down.

Playful Poems

Saigyō also composed a type of poetry he called *tawabure uta*, "playful poems." These poems lie completely outside the bounds of contemporary court poetry. Late in life, while living in the Saga area of Kyoto, he composed a number of them. They are all favorites of mine, and I can recite nearly all of them by heart.

unaiko ga	A young child
susami ni narasu	at play with
mugibue no	a straw whistle—
koe ni odoroku	the sound startles me awake
natsu no hirubushi	from my summer afternoon nap.

One hot summer afternoon, Saigyō is napping inside his hut when he is awakened by a shrill piping sound. He looks around and realizes it is from an *unaiko*, a child young enough to wear its hair bound at the back of the neck, playing innocently with a straw whistle. The scene is extremely pleasant: a hot afternoon; Saigyō, an old man, peacefully dozing; just as he is about to awaken, a shrill sound startles him into full alertness; he looks around in surprise and sees a small child tootling on a straw whistle in the sizzling heat. Picturing the scene always fills me with contentment. The scene in the poem arises out of a heart that is as empty as the sky. Unconcerned with poetic techniques or the nature of beauty, Saigyō is prepared to accept whatever arises before him, which is what enables him to capture moments such as this. This is the same as the spirit of Zen.

In another poem I love, the poet enters straight into a child's heart. Septuagenarian Saigyō fondly recalls his boyhood while looking affectionately at a young boy at play:

shino tamete	Using cut bamboo

suzume yumi haru	to fashion a bow
o no warawa	for shooting sparrows,
hitai eboshi no	the boy longs for
hoshige naru kana	the headgear of a warrior.

A small boy has cut bamboo grass and is now bending it to form a bow with which to shoot at sparrows. Perhaps doing so makes him feel strong, for he seems to be wishing he had a small *eboshi*, the headgear of a warrior. It would become him very well, thinks the poet.

itaki kana	How splendid!
shōbu kaburi no	And to think this iris-crowned
chimaki uma wa	toy horse of straw
unai warawa no	was fashioned by the hands
shiwaza to oboete	of a little child!

A *chimaki uma* is a horse made of *kaya*, the grass used for thatching roofs. The poet marvels at how dexterously the toy horse is made and wonders if it could really be the handiwork of a young child. That's all there is to this poem, but it is very agreeable.

takeuma o	Stilts today
tsue ni mo kyō wa	would be for me
tanomu kana	a pair of canes—
warawa asobi o	remembering
omoi idetsutsu	childhood play.

Children are at play, using stilts. If the poet were to use stilts today, they could only function as canes, but he remembers vividly what it was like to be a child.

Not one other poet in Saigyō's circle of contemporaries ever would or could have thought of composing such poems. Only Saigyō could have written them. That is because his heart is empty of all preconceived notions of what poetry is or must be. His heartstrings were always taut, so when anything touched them, the result was a poem.

Evaluating Saigyō

Retired emperor Gotoba acknowledged Saigyō's greatness. He led the team of poets who spent years assembling the eighth imperial *waka* anthology and was said to know by heart almost every one of the 1,900 entries, so his knowledge of poetry is beyond question. His critiques of various leading poets of the day, which are gathered in a book called *Secret Teachings of the Retired Emperor Gotoba*, are fascinating and brilliant. He reserves his highest praise for Saigyō: "Saigyō's works are interesting and expressive of unusually deep feeling, combined with a rare originality. I believe he is a born poet. Ordinary people should not try to learn from him. His superiority is beyond description." Run-of-the-mill poets should not try to model themselves on Saigyō, he says; to do so they would need a mind equal to Saigyō's and a similarly profound mastery of language. Efforts of lesser poets will end in disaster. The retired sovereign accurately grasped the nature of Saigyō's genius, and his judgment was passed on to later generations.

As I mentioned earlier, Bashō was an ardent admirer of Saigyō. On the occasion of the transfer of one Morikawa Kyoriku from Edo to Hikone in the fourth month of 1693, Bashō wrote a farewell entitled "The Rustic Gate," another work I am much taken with. In his parting words, he says this: "Even in the poems of Saigyō that were lightly tossed off, there is much that is moving. Did not the retired emperor Gotoba say his poems contain truth tinged with sorrow? Take strength from these words and follow the narrow path of poetry without swerving." The reference to poems "lightly tossed off" suggests the spirit of the "playful poems." What's interesting here is that Gotoba never actually wrote one word about Saigyō's words being "tinged with sorrow." Somehow his commentary was transformed in Bashō's mind. The transmission of literary culture takes mysterious turns: Bashō venerated Saigyō and concurred with Gotoba's assessment of him, but somehow he internalized that assessment in his own way. "Truth tinged with sorrow" is surely Bashō's own highest ideal, and in his mind that is how the ex-emperor's praise was rendered.

Gotoba's book was intended to teach would-be poets how to write poetry in line with the conventions of the day. Saigyō's poetry, however, is unconventional. He breaks rules of the day by repeating words consecutively and using colloquial language, yet at the same time produces magnificent poetry. He is a genius, which is precisely why Gotoba warns beginners against mimicking him. The freedom of Saigyō's verse is an indication of the freedom with which he lived.

Following the Heart

Saigyō lived during a tumultuous time that saw the emergence of two rival warrior clans, the Heike and the Genji, with severe discord and fighting that ended in the establishment of Japan's first military government, the Kamakura shogunate. Yet despite his close ties to the political authority of the court, Saigyō paid no attention to such goings-on and merely followed the dictates of his heart.

Emperor Toba was forced to abdicate at age twenty in favor of his young son, Emperor Sutoku. But Sutoku was said to have been fathered not by Toba but by retired emperor Shirakawa, the child emperor's supposed grandfather. Toba loathed Sutoku and called him "Ojiko," literally "uncle child," or "not mine but his grandfather's offspring."

Before Saigyō became a monk, when he was still a warrior in the northern Fujiwara clan, retired emperor Toba was his sovereign. Moreover, Sutoku's mother, Fujiwara no Shōshi, was a member of the Tokudaiji family that Saigyō served early in life. He had profound respect for her and, according to some accounts, may even have been in love with her. In short, he had intimate connections to the family of retired emperor Toba and felt an affinity to Emperor Sutoku, who was just one year his junior and also a knowledgeable and gifted poet. Despite all this, Saigyō never sided with either Toba or Sutoku.

In 1156, when Toba died at the age of fifty-four, Saigyō attended the funeral. Six days later, the Hōgen disturbance broke out as rival factions in the court fought for the succession through their respective lines, involving samurai forces in the dispute. Sutoku was defeated and exiled to Sanuki Province on Shikoku, a bitter fate. Saigyō wrote the following poem at age thirty-nine, seventeen years after the visit referred to in the headnote: "Retired emperor Toba passed away, and as they were taking his remains to the Imperial Palace I came down from Mount Takano and happened to encounter the funeral procession. It was very sad. I remembered the old days at Toba Detached Palace, which the retired emperor first saw when he went there for a preliminary inspection. I accompanied him, along with Minister of the Right Tokudaiji no Saneyoshi. Filled with sorrowful memories, I wrote this poem."

koyoi koso	Tonight indeed
omoi shirarure	it has come home to me
asakaranu	how deep the bond
kimi ni chigiri no	I shared with you, how strong
aru mi narikeri	the pledge between us.

His fondness for the departed sovereign drew him straight to the funeral procession and filled him with grief as he remembered the time they had spent at Toba Detached Palace, a magnificent complex begun by retired emperor Shirakawa in 1086 and later expanded by retired emperor Toba and others. He did this in full awareness of the discord between Toba and Sutoku.

On the occasion of Sutoku's banishment after starting the Hōgen disturbance and suffering ignominious defeat, Saigyō wrote the following poem, with the explanatory headnote "A serious matter occurred and the retired emperor was subjected to an unthinkable fate, after which he shaved his head and entered Ninnaji temple. On hearing that, I went there, and the eminent priest Kengen came out and met me. I composed this poem under a bright moon":

kakaru yo ni	In such a world
kage mo kawarazu	the moon alone is clear,
sumu tsuki o	its light unchanging,
miru waga mi sae	and I who gaze upon it
urameshiki kana	am filled with sorrow.

Saigyō loved the retired emperor Sutoku. He felt close to him. He also looked up to the retired emperor Toba. Even though their separate factions clashed, he retained high regard for both men—certainly a politically dangerous stance, yet he never wavered. He remained true to his feelings and treated the bitter rivals with equal respect.

Years later, on hearing that after his banishment Sutoku let his hair and nails grow long, acquiring the appearance of a demon, Saigyō wrote a poem taking him to task. After Sutoku passed away, he went to Shikoku and prayed for his soul. These actions are testimony to Saigyō's sincerity, kindness, and indifference to politics, attributes that only increase my admiration for him.

20

Seeing the Afterlife Close at Hand

"What is this fighting all about?"

Saigyō's actions suggest that he was apolitical, or not bound by such aspects of earthly life as politics. He behaved with great freedom. Both when composing poetry and in the way he lived his life, Saigyō was true to himself, conducting himself always in accord with his deepest instincts and not allowing anything to hold him back. In renouncing the world he became free: herein lies his greatness.

As we know, Saigyō lived during the era of violent clashes known as the Gempei War, based on the rivalry of the Minamoto (Genji) and Taira (Heike) houses. Having been born in the same year as the powerful leader Taira no Kiyomori, he might have been sympathetic to the Heike side, but he never said so. Unlike other poets of his circle, he did not shy away from issues of politics, famine, or other unpleasant realities. Here is one example. The headnote reads "Warriors rose in society and now strife is everywhere: north, south, east, and west. The number of dead one hears of is staggering, so many that it scarcely seems real. What is this fighting all about? Written on thinking how pitiable humanity is."

Shide no yama   On Death Mountain,

koyuru taema wa	people cross over

koyuru taema wa   people cross over
araji kashi   without end—
nakunaru hito no   the number of the dying
kazu tsuzukitsutsu   continues to grow.

The headnote to the poem seems to spring straight from his heart. The warrior class, formerly held back by the court nobles, has been gaining in strength. On all sides, warriors are fighting among themselves. Just as recounted in *Tales of the Heike*, there has been battle after battle, and Saigyō, staggered by the number of dead, cannot understand why such fighting has to take place. To fight over power or wealth, and to kill one another for such things, strikes him as sheer madness. The poem expresses his heart-sickness at the sad spectacle.

To escape chaos and strife, Saigyō took up residence in Futamigaura, Ise, where he would live for several years. A Shinto priest named Ozaki Mitsuyoshi, who later became his disciple and took the monastic name Ren'a, recorded his teachings in a book called *Conversations with Saigyō*, written some thirty years after Saigyō's death. Ren'a observed Saigyō close at hand and describes his lifestyle in detail. Saigyō lived in a brushwood hut that was simple yet elegant, the sort of place that purifies the soul and refreshes the spirit. Ren'a records details such as the inkstone he used, a very ordinary one. He writes, "The master used to say that composing poetry is purifying to the heart, so that evil thoughts do not arise and one is drawn into the state of mind that contemplates the afterlife. This is certainly true." In other words, Saigyō saw the way of poetry as one with the way of Buddhism.

Saigyō lamented the constant fighting of the time, which took place for reasons he could not fathom. He himself was of warrior stock, had begun life a warrior, so he could not look on unmoved at the deaths of so many warriors. He had renounced that way of life and given himself over to the service of the Buddha, but the others of his class had not. They remained warriors whose fate it was to fight and to die in battle. Saigyō's poem "On Death Mountain" rose from his mixed feelings as he contemplated their deaths.

This series of poems is included in *Things Heard and Noted*, just after the series written after viewing a hell-screen; the hell those poems refer to seems to overlap with the hellish fighting in this world. The next poem bears this headnote: "An unending swarm of warriors crosses Death Mountain. With so many warriors about, there would be no fear of mountain bandits, if it were in this world. There was something called the battle of Uji, where he remembered hearing they crossed the river on horse rafts." This comment is tinged with irony.

The battle of Uji did take place as described; Heike troops crossed the rough Uji River by fastening horses together like rafts. In *Tales of the Heike* this scene comes in the fourth volume, titled "The Battle at the Bridge." Here is how the epic describes the instructions given by Ashikaga no Matatarō Tadatsuna of Shimotsuke Province:

> Put the strong horses upstream and the weak ones downstream. As long as they can stand, let them walk with slack reins. When they begin to thrash around, tighten the reins to make them swim. If someone falls behind, have him catch hold of your bow. Hold hands, stand shoulder to shoulder while you cross. Sit tight in the saddle and plant your feet in the stirrups. Pull your horse's head up if it goes under the water, but not too hard.

In this fashion, the warriors safely crossed the river on horse rafts. Of the more than three hundred troops, not one was swept away and lost. This scene is one of the highlights of *Tales of the Heike*. Saigyō, recalling this scene, wrote the following poem.

Illustrated Hand-scroll of Tales of the Heike, "Bridge Battle" (detail), Hayashibara Museum of Art

shizumu naru	On Death Mountain
Shide no yamagawa	the river overflows with dead
minagirite	being swept away;
umaikade mo ya	a raft of horses here
kanawazaru ramu	would be of little use.

Furthermore, Saigyō memorialized the death of the young Minamoto general Kiso no Yoshinaka in this poem, with the curt headnote "A warrior named Kiso has died."

Kisobito wa	The man from Kiso
umi no ikari o	unable to still
shizumekanete	the raging sea
Shide no yama ni mo	has made his way
iri ni keru kana	to Death Mountain.

The poem contains a play on words, as *ikari* means both "rage" and "anchor." The "man from Kiso" entered Death Mountain because he lost the sea battle; sea and land (mountain) form a contrast.

In all three poems, Saigyō maintains a distance from the fighting itself. Viewed from the perspective of Buddhism, all fighting in this world is foolishness. Saigyō views it from afar; his comment on the death of Yoshinaka seems particularly aloof. In any case, the heartfelt query "What is this conflict all about?" reveals Saigyō's disdain for the conflicts of his day.

Japan's involvement in war is now fading from living memory, but from 1941 to 1945 we fought against the United States in World War II and before that we engaged China in a futile war. Like Saigyō in this poem, I too resented the war and wondered why I had to be caught up in it and perhaps die. People in the center of such adversity are unable to see the point of it. Perhaps that is the nature of history.

Second Journey to Michinoku

In 1186, at what was then the extremely advanced age of sixty-nine, Saigyō set out once again for Michinoku in the far northeast. The reason for his expedition had roots in events that took place years before. In late 1180, Taira no Shigehira, Kiyomori's fifth son, advanced on Nara with troops and set fire to homes to quell riots by armed monks at Tōdaiji monastery. In the process, an unlucky gust of wind caused the fire to destroy not only Tōdaiji but also Kōfukuji, the family temple of the Fujiwara. The 1536 *History of the Tōdaiji Great Buddha Hall* contains a detailed description of the scene, recounting how elderly monks and scholar monks fled to the top floor of the hall of the Great Buddha, only to be burned alive in a ghastly inferno. Saigyō made the journey north at the request of the monk Chōgen, who was overseeing the rebuilding of Tōdaiji and wanted Saigyō to raise funds from his northern Fujiwara relatives.

The poems that Saigyō composed along the way are, I think, among his masterpieces. Around this time, Japan remained in considerable turmoil. The violent Gempei War had just ended with the collapse of the Heike. Minamoto no Yoshitsune, who had done the most to defeat the Heike, incurred the wrath of his older brother, Yoritomo, who was hunting him down. Yoshitsune's lover Shizuka was in Kamakura, a captive.

Fujiwara no Hidehira, head of the Northern Fujiwara family, was the powerful ruler of Mutsu Province, lord of Mutsu and commander in chief of the defense of the north. He played a critical role in Yoshitsune's early life, sheltering him in a temple on Mt. Kurama, just north of Kyoto, till he was fifteen. When Yoshitsune learned that his brother had raised an army, he overcame Hidehira's objections and ran off to join him.

In this way, there was a surprising link between Saigyō and Yoshitsune, through the poet's blood connection to Hidehira. Yoritomo, holding the reins of power in Kamakura, suspected that Hidehira would again offer Yoshitsune shelter and was keeping a close watch. Saigyō's trip took place under these perilous conditions, conditions that he was certainly fully aware of. Step by step, he drew closer to the far northeastern land, sensing danger as he went.

Saigyō's earlier journey to Michinoku had taken place in his late twenties. For him to undertake the same journey at sixty-nine must have brought on deep emotion, as seen in the following poem. The headnote reads "Heading east to visit an acquaintance, I passed Mt. Sayanonaka, where I had been before. I remembered that time, now so long ago."

toshi takete	Never did I think
mata koyu beshi to	at my advanced old age
omoiki ya	to cross here again,
inochi narikeri	but this is my life—
Sayanonakayama	Mt. Sayanonaka.

The words "my life" have great weight. Saigyō has defied all expectations by crossing this mountain again in old age. Being alive has allowed this amazing thing to happen. He has been alive for seven decades, and now, thanks to Mt. Sayanonaka, he has this chance to look back on his life. The words "my life" signify his entire lifetime, and from the poem we understand the solemnity he feels on contemplating his life. It is a masterful poem.

Here is another poem worthy of high praise; it is the sort of poem a person could compose only once in a lifetime. The headnote reads "On a journey east for spiritual discipline, on seeing Mt. Fuji."

kaze ni nabiku	Trailing on the wind,
Fuji no kemuri no	smoke from Mt. Fuji
sora ni kiete	fades into the sky,
yukue mo shiranu	drifting toward an unknown end
waga omoi kana	just like my own thoughts.

At the time, Fuji was an active volcano. The season is autumn, I imagine, and in a cloudless sky of clear blue, smoke from the peak drifts on the wind and vanishes into the empty sky, its destination unknowable. In the same way, the poet's thoughts—his life, we may as well say—drifts away with the distant clouds, to what end he does not know. The smoke from Mt. Fuji represents his own journeying heart. Where do the workings of his mind vanish to? There is no telling. The poet's life as an individual merges with the life of the universe as, while looking at the actual scene in front of him, he glimpses eternity. The landscape in nature overlaps with the landscape of his own mind. This superb poem achieves the coalescence of human life and nature.

As I mentioned before, when Saigyō died, leading poets of the day wrote poems mourning him. Here is a moving one by Jien:

kaze ni nabiku	He who likened himself
Fuji no keburi ni	to Fuji's smoke
tagui ni shi	trailing on the wind—
hito no yukue wa	where he has gone
sora ni shirarete	the sky alone knows.

Jien wrote in his *Collection of Gathered Gems* that Saigyō considered "Trailing on the wind" to be his finest work; apparently his contemporaries also recognized it as the poem of his lifetime.

Saigyō and Yoritomo

Finally, Saigyō went to Kamakura. He probably had no particular motive in going there, but his presence happened to draw the eye of the shogun. The historical chronicle *Mirror of the East* gives an invaluable account of Saigyō's encounter with Yoritomo in an entry for the fifteenth day of the eighth month, 1186. The following is my paraphrase of the classical text.

It was the fifteenth day of the eighth month, already autumn. When Shogun Yoritomo visited Tsurugaoka Shrine, he saw an old monk wandering around by the *torii* gate. Normally he would have paid little attention, but something about the old monk's appearance and demeanor caught his eye. Yoritomo became curious and had Sasaki Kagesue go and ask his name. The monk said he used to be called Satō Norikiyo and now went by the name of Saigyō. Yoritomo recognized the name, and after worshiping at the shrine he sent a message saying he would like to have a quiet meeting and inquire about poetry. Saigyō accepted the invitation. After that Yoritomo went around to other shrines and temples, performing acts of devotion. As soon as he returned home, he sent for Saigyō and quizzed him about poetry as well as archery and horsemanship. Saigyō said that when he was a layman, his skills with the bow and horses, requirements for any military man, were so lackluster that he was barely able to keep up the family traditions in martial arts. He was the ninth-generation heir of Fujiwara Hidesato, whose military knowhow had been passed down all those generations, but when he renounced the world and became a priest during the eighth month of 1137 he burned the family secrets, so they were lost forever. As such matters were a source of sin for one who had entered the priesthood, he had never given them another thought, and all his knowledge in that realm had passed into oblivion. Concerning the composition of poetry, all he did was put his emotions into thirty-one syllables upon being stirred by cherry blossoms or the moon. He had no deep mysteries to share.

This was quite a brusque response: a profession of ignorance about all three fields, including poetry. However, Saigyō was probably being honest. His poetry was uncontrived. He simply kept his heart polished, and when moved by cherry blossoms or the moon, would compose a verse. As he told the monk Myōe, he belonged to the Shingon sect of Buddhism, but this information he didn't share with Yoritomo.

Not content with this reply, Yoritomo probed him further about archery and equestrian skills. Saigyō then did reveal various things. Yoritomo had a man named Toshikane take down what he said, and that record survives, but unfortunately I have not yet read it. The next morning, Yoritomo presented Saigyō with a cat figurine made of silver. Saigyō accepted the gift, but once beyond the gate he handed it to a child at play.

This incident is, I think, highly revealing of Saigyō's style. Yoritomo, the ruler of the land, meant nothing to him. He paid him no notice whatever. He himself must have had a dignified, intrepid appearance for Yoritomo to have entertained him with such consideration. History gives rise to many fascinating moments. This passage shines a welcome spotlight on a chapter of Saigyō's life and showcases his powerful spirit so vividly that we can almost picture him.

Yosa Buson

1716–1784

Buson, *Blossom Viewing*,
Itsuō Art Museum

A haiku poet and Nanga painter. Born in Settsu Province (present-day southeastern Hyōgo and northern Osaka Prefectures), he had the original surname of Taniguchi, later Yosa. At around age 21 he went to Edo, where he studied *haikai,* the precursor of haiku, becoming the pupil of Hayano (Yahantei) Hajin while simultaneously pursuing Nanga. After Hajin's death, he traveled around northern Kantō and parts farther north, devoting himself to painting. From autumn 1751 he lived in Kyoto, then in a succession of places including the town of Yosa, Tango Province, developing a unique style. Later he again took up *haikai,* and in 1770 assumed his former master's pen-name. He established the "Tenmei-era *haikai*" movement, advocating a return to the style of Bashō. His main works are found in the following collections: *Buson kushū* (Haiku of Buson), *Shin hanatsumi* (New flower picking) and *Yahanraku* (Midnight music). He also left many paintings, including a famous collaborative work done with Ike no Taiga (1723–1776).

21

A Haiku Poet of Grand Vistas

Grand Vistas

We turn now to a discussion of the haiku poet Yosa Buson, but first, at the risk of repeating myself, I would like to emphasize that I am not a scholar of Japanese literature. I am merely someone who enjoys the classics as an amateur. My discussions contain no groundbreaking interpretations or new theories. But I have long admired the celebrated haiku of Buson, and here I would like to offer some of my favorites for others to appreciate as well.

Let's get started with Buson's most famous haiku.

haru no umi	Spring sea—
hinemosu notari	all day long the waves
notari kana	gently rise and fall

While the poem evokes a bright, relaxed image of spring, when I murmur it to myself it brings to mind a rather sad if fond memory. When I was growing up, compulsory education ended with the sixth grade. In 1937, of my sixth-grade class of fifty, fewer than ten went on to a five-year middle school. The rest of us either joined the work force or stayed on for an additional two years before becoming home helpers, office boys, factory hands, apprentices, or what have you. The prewar educational system was cruel in that respect. Denied access to higher education, my unfortunate classmates and I were pretty down in the mouth.

One day we encountered Buson's "Spring sea" in our textbook. Back then, rather than having pupils hash out the meaning of what they read, teachers focused on recitation. You had to read aloud in a clear, strong voice. (I have to say it was a fine teaching method; constantly quizzing students on meaning the way they do nowadays doesn't foster a love of reading.) The classmate who was called on to read managed to muff it in a spectacular way. The class howled with laughter. I laughed too, and yet for some reason I was sad.

Over six decades later, I still remember that day. The haiku has grandeur, I believe, in its portrayal of the relaxed, expansive movement of the sea in spring. But as a child, my friend's blunder somehow made me write off the poem as too obvious and lacking depth. It took me a long time to learn to appreciate it, but now I believe it fully encapsulates Buson's greatness.

Modern haiku poets take pleasure in delicate emotions and no longer compose haiku so grand in scale, nor do they value them particularly highly. Buson is second to none in his ability to paint scenes of cosmic scale in a mere seventeen syllables.

This one has the headnote "Spring scenery":

na no hana ya	Rape flowers—
tsuki wa higashi ni	the moon in the east,
hi wa nishi ni	the sun in the west

On first reading, this haiku also seems simple, but the scene it portrays is vast, containing both sun and moon. In Buson's day, western Japan produced rapeseed oil in great quantity and rape-flower cultivation was big business. Here, as the poet walks in an immense field of yellow blossoms, before him the sun tilts west, bathing the scene in sunset hues. He glances behind him and sees the moon looming large at the horizon. Again, I didn't think much of the poem when I was young; I couldn't see what was so remarkable about it. But as I grew older, I came to realize that poems like this are actually more difficult to write than poems of smaller scale. To paint a scene this vast with utter simplicity and no letup of tension requires enormous capability.

Kakinomoto no Hitomaro, the seventh-century poet featured most prominently in the ancient anthology *Ten Thousand Leaves*, wrote this celebrated *waka*:

himukashi no	Over eastern fields
no ni kagiroi no	I watch the morning
tatsu miete	flame up
kaerimi sureba	then turn and see
tsuki katabukinu	the moon tilting west.

Here the scene is morning, the opposite of Buson's haiku, but in terms of scale the two are a match. I can't help liking that Buson wrote expansive haiku such as this, ones that show him to be Hitomaro's full equal.

The next haiku is arresting.

na no hana ya	Rape flowers—
kujira mo yorazu	no whales draw near as
umi kurenu	the sea darkens

Why did Buson bring in whales? Surely he wasn't expecting any to show up. The setting is a seaside field of rape at twilight. Minus the looming presence of any giant whales, the sea darkens in tranquility. The reference to nonexistent whales is fascinating. Buson uses his imagination to evoke whales by their absence, a technique that modern haiku poets eschew. The modern tendency is to value realism above all else, although in my opinion slavish devotion to realism makes for insipid poetry. Buson freely weaves in everything from slang expressions and products of his imagination to history and legend, creating a world of incredible richness. If modern haiku poets continue their relentless insistence on realism, I fear the genre will be steadily impoverished.

Buson's power of imagination is splendid. When he looks at a scene or vista, he doesn't compose a haiku based directly on what's in front of his eyes, but first dips it in his poetical imagination—the store of poetry in his heart, the mother lode of poetry.

hōhyakuri	For a hundred leagues square
amagumo yosenu	holding rainclouds at bay—
botamu kana	the peony

To convey the gorgeousness of the peony blossom, he starts out with "one hundred leagues square," a distance the mind can't easily wrap itself around. In some contexts the word *yosenu* could mean "has brought near" or "summoned," but here it means rather "holds off, keeps away." The peony has the power to hold rainclouds at bay for a hundred leagues in all directions. The dignity and beauty of the bloom are exaggerated to highly pleasing effect. Who else has written haiku like this? Some may be put off by this style, but I like it very much.

Fuji hitotsu	Only Mt. Fuji
uzumi nokoshite	left unengulfed—
wakaba kana	the lush young leaves

This verse too is grand in scale. All around are young green leaves, and Mt.

Fuji alone rises from their midst, perhaps still capped with snow. Again Buson is using hyperbole; this could hardly be called a "sketch from life." I once read a commentary suggesting that the scene is an aerial view, but to me that seems unlikely. I think the poem is best appreciated by imagining a world filled with lush green leaves of early summer, where, in the sole space not overtaken, Mt. Fuji rises in lonely majesty. Buson uses nontraditional characters for the name of the mountain, choosing to write it so the meaning becomes "matchless." The leaves have spread everywhere except where the matchless mountain, Mt. Fuji, rises.

Buson wrote many other haiku in a similar vein, including this one with the headnote "Returning from Naniwa with Takai Kitō":

shimo hyakuri	Frost for a hundred leagues—
shūchū ni ware	alone in my boat
tsuki o ryōsu	I rule the moon

This is a poem about a boat ride down the Yodo River. Frost lies over all, as far as the eye can see, and the moon lights up the scene. The actual distance involved is a mere thirteen leagues, but Buson exaggerates it all the way to one hundred. Alone in his boat, he rules this vast world. This poem too is cheerful and invigorating.

Buson's Sense of Space

The following haiku is a great favorite of mine.

tsuki tenshin	High overhead
mazushiki machi o	the moon, passing above
tōri keri	this wretched town

Buson, *Snowclad Houses in the Night*, Private collection

This is one of Buson's most celebrated poems, establishing a connection between the moon traversing the vastness of the sky above and what I imagine to be the poet's own small dwelling in the dilapidated town below. *Tsuki tenshin* apparently refers to the meteorological phenomenon whereby in winter the moon occupies the center of the sky; around the winter solstice, the full moon is at its highest at midnight. The verse suggests a town in winter in the dead of night, its inhabitants asleep in their beds while the moon in the middle of the sky sheds its radiance over all. Just overhead, the full moon lights up the impoverished town as it sails over small, shabby houses with roofs of wooden planks held down by stones.

Tōri keri, "passing above," I take as Buson's personal experience. He didn't become a renowned haiku master until his mid-fifties, before which time he was virtually unknown. Once past the age of fifty he began to write haiku in great numbers. (I feel that I too came into my own past the age of fifty, so I feel a bond with Buson.) Earlier in life he traveled east to Kantō and endured considerable poverty and suffering. The haiku could be referring to those experiences, but that's not all. The way I see it, he is living

alone in "this wretched town" as the shimmering moon passes above. The contrast between the bright full moon of winter, so close overhead, and the wretched town below, bathed in moonlight, is extremely beautiful.

Buson wrote a number of other haiku with similar spatial perspectives:

uzumibi ya	Banked fire—
waga kakurega mo	my hermitage likewise
yuki no naka	buried in the snow

In the cold winter night, he probably has his arms around a hibachi for warmth. Deep within the hibachi are red-hot coals buried in ash. Similarly, he himself is snug inside a house buried in snow. Above the snow stretch the dark, unknowable reaches of the sky. The haiku focuses on the banked fire and above it the poet, above the poet his house, and above the whole scene the universe—all of it grasped simultaneously in a few syllables.

This haiku reminds me of Buson's famous horizontal scroll painting *Snowclad Houses in the Night*. White mountains occupy the center of the painting, and spreading out from the foothills is an array of humble houses, with here and there a taller structure, all with snow-piled roofs. The viewer is looking down on the scene. Here, too, Buson is in one of the houses, warming his chapped hands at a banked fire. There is a similar progression from the burning embers to himself, the house, and the world spread out beneath a vast sky. The poet feels connected with the universe. Both the scroll painting and the haiku suggest the limitless expanse of night.

Layers of Time

As we have seen, in his haiku Buson often places himself in an infinitesimally small nook while simultaneously evoking a sense of overreaching vastness. He does something similar with time, deftly weighing time past or future from his perspective in the here and now. No one comes close to Buson, I think, in his ability to evoke time's flow or seriality.

> *harusame ya*   Spring rain
> *kurenan to shite*   the day ending—
> *kyō mo ari*   I linger too

This wonderful haiku is typical. Spring rain falls softly and steadily while the poet sits idly at home, listening. The days are growing longer, and this one is slowly drawing to a close. Normal order for the second and third lines would be the less interesting *kyō mo kurenan/to shite ari*, literally "today is drawing to a close." Inversion gives the final line the sense that "today I also exist," with the poet as implied subject. Words are strange things, changing their meaning by such subtle shifts. Not only today is lingering; I too am lingering, in and with the long, rainy spring day. I savor the remnants of the day, savoring the delicacy of the spring rain as evening sets in, aware simultaneously of the passage of a day and of my life: because I am alive now, I can sit and appreciate this moment in time. This haiku was composed when Buson was sixty-seven; by layering the sense of time, overlapping the waning of his life with the slow end of a rainy day in spring, he evokes a sense of the infinite.

The next poem forms the basis of the sensibility in the previous one. Again, the waning of life is enveloped in the softness of an evening in spring. The headnote reads "Longing for the past":

kinō kure	Yesterday ended,
kyō mata kurete	today is also ending—
yuku haru ya	so goes the spring

Yesterday drew to a close and now today is ending too; I remember yesterday, and I am now appreciating this day too, realizing it will soon disappear, feeling as if I am afloat in eternity.

Next is another famous haiku, a truly fine work:

osoki hi no	Lazy spring days
tsumorite tōki	piling up—so far away,
mukashi kana	the past

"Lazy days" is a standard reference to spring; the winter is over and spring lingers on with no sign of ending any time soon. As the days pile up, they seem to stretch back all the way to the distant past, filling the poet with memories both tender and sad. He remembers people from long ago, their faces coming back to him one by one, but he himself has grown old, and all those with whom he might have spoken of those days are gone. Here again the poet's awareness of the present moment, as the spring evening wears on, forms the background of the poem. Such moments, such evenings, pile up in layers like thin membranes, turning to memories that carry him far into the past. Time past is linked to and contiguous with time present; the poet's gaze is fixed simultaneously on eternity and now.

Concerning this haiku, the poet Nagisao Yajima has written, "The superlative skill shown in this poem lies in the presentation of formless time as something tangible that can 'accumulate'; in the rendering of something invisible as visible."[21] This is clearly so. We are intuitively drawn by the presentation of time as multilayered, something "piling up, so far away."

These haiku are filled with nostalgia. Buson was inordinately fond of spring evenings, and I would say that poems such as these qualify him to be known as a supreme "poet of nostalgia."

---

21 Yajima Nagisao, *Yosa Buson sansaku* (Tokyo: Kadokawa Shoten, 1995).

22

Poems of Deep Feeling

Classical Allusions and Shared Culture

We have already examined some of Buson's most famous haiku, and here is one more on the passing of spring.

yuku haru ya	The passing spring—
omotaki biwa no	the lute in my arms
dakigokoro	weighs heavy

Japanese people feel sorrow at the passing of spring, a sorrow well expressed in this haiku. The one embracing the lute may be Buson himself, or it may be a courtier of the ancient Heian era. Filled with languor and melancholy at the waning of spring, he feels the instrument weighing heavy in his arms. Though I personally have never held a lute, through this poem I can share the scene and the mood with distant ancestors. Mournfulness at the passing of spring is connected to sadness at the slipping away of one's own life on the journey toward death, and here the one filled with such poignant thoughts clasps a musical instrument in his arms. It is a beautiful image. As readers, we nurture our spirits through repeated appreciation of such moments.

Classics are the intermediaries through which we create ourselves. Discovery of the classics enables us to share the values of distant generations and adopt them as our own. When we find something we love, whether it be prose or poetry, that passage or idea takes root within us and becomes internalized as our culture, providing strength and support. Yet unfortunately, young people today seldom read books—a state I find unimaginable—much less the classics. I worry about what will happen to our shared culture.

During the Tokugawa period, members of the samurai class, as well as townsmen with a desire to study, read the *Analects* and other works. They didn't pick Confucius' words apart by reading commentaries and trying to interpret the meaning, but committed them to memory. Even little children piped passages written in classical style: "To learn and from time to time review what you have learned, is this not a pleasure?" Because they read and memorized the same things, Tokugawa-period Japanese shared the same values. Even if the dialects they spoke were so different as to make oral communication nearly impossible, as between the people of Satsuma in the south and Tohoku in the north, they shared the same culture based on common values. This explains why, at the time of the Meiji Restoration of 1868, people of Japan's north and south were able to come together and trust one another.

What Japan needs most right now is the desire to seek and share a culture based on those timeless values. Buson's haiku on the passing of spring makes me feel that need more strongly than ever.

Daily Life in Haiku

Onitsura ya   Onitsura—
shinshu no naka no in the season of new saké
bin ni shosu   at ease in poverty

Uejima Onitsura, a famous haiku poet active in the Osaka region in the early eighteenth century, was born the son of a wealthy saké brewer in Itami (present-day Hyogo Prefecture). He was fond of *haikai* (linked verse) and, despite his affluent origins, devoted his life to composing verses in poverty. Now it is "the season of new saké," the busiest time of year for brewers, yet Onitsura is leading a life of leisure in his poverty.

Buson earned a living by painting, but he doubtless identified with Onitsura. As his fame as a haiku poet grew, more and more people came clamoring to be taken on as his disciples, but he always turned them down, preferring to remain poor rather than busy himself with paying students. Buson mingled only with people on the same level as him, so his family never escaped poverty.

Matsuo Bashō, whom Buson revered, was the same. He wrote in *Knapsack Notebook,* "At last, having no ability or skill, I followed this one course"—the path of *haikai.* He gave his life to literary art, not knowing whether he had any talent to speak of. This approach sums up the admirable spirit of old-time men of letters in Japan. We who are involved in literary and artistic pursuits today should take Bashō's words to heart.

ayu kurete	You brought sweetfish
yorade sugiyuku	but didn't stay to visit—
yowa no kado	the gate at midnight

This is a simple haiku of deep feeling, one that I like very much. Someone pounds on the gate late at night, and when the poet goes out to see who it is, his friend hands him some freshly-caught sweetfish and then quickly takes his leave, not wanting to cause any bother. This is the thoughtful behavior captured in the haiku, which strikes me as portraying a beautiful gesture of friendship. Reading it makes me happy.

Buson wrote all sorts of haiku about daily life, including the following famous one:

sararetaru	The divorced woman
mi o fungonde	strides into the field
taue kana	to plant rice seedlings

A husband used to be able to divorce his wife simply by furnishing a written statement of divorce that consisted of a mere 3½ lines. That is apparently what happened to the woman in this haiku. However, planting rice seedlings in the wet rice fields required the participation of all members of every household, and so, despite her shame and embarrassment at having been cast aside, she has no choice but to take her place. The word "strides" indicates her determination and spirit. Reading this haiku, I picture the face of a plucky woman—the sort of woman who must have been common in old Japan. The historical fiction of the late Fujisawa Shūhei, all of whose works I have read with much pleasure, depicts strong women who say little and keep their feelings to themselves, bearing their burdens quietly. The divorced woman in this haiku is like them.

The following haiku has a somewhat similar flavor.

oteuchi no	Once condemned to die
meoto narishi o	husband and wife now enjoy
koromogae	the seasonal change of wardrobe

During the Tokugawa period, two people serving in the same samurai household were not permitted to marry, a rule that often led to sexual misconduct—a crime punishable by death. The young couple in this haiku were sentenced to die by the sword, but the daimyo relented and allowed them to live quietly in town as husband and wife. Today is the day in summer when everyone changes to warm-weather clothes, a day of new beginning. The two of them are full of joy at being alive and able to share this special day, fresh and clean. Whether Buson was writing about an actual incident or from imagination doesn't matter. The important thing is that he packed such a complex situation, with all its hidden undercurrents, into seventeen syllables. The custom of changing wardrobe with the season takes on added meaning by its association with this revitalized couple.

Since I myself have grown old, Buson's haiku on old age resonate more than ever with me. This one makes me feel a certain chagrin:

toshimoru yo	Year-end watch—
oi wa tōtoku	tonight we aged ones
miraretari	are held in honor

The year is ending, and everyone has gathered on the last night of the year to sit up and see in the new year—originally a Chinese custom, apparently. On this night the elderly are held in especially high regard. It is gratifying to know that this was once the custom. Today, all too often oldsters are made to feel in the way.

And then I come upon a haiku like this:

hana tarete	Nose dripping
hitori go o utsu	playing go all alone
yozamu kana	on a cold night

This one brings me even greater chagrin. The poet is playing the game of go alone, without a companion. He is probably not challenging himself to a game but more likely following model games played by masters, collected in a book. I too do this frequently, as I love the game of go. I get involved in the moves without realizing the temperature is dropping, and before I know it, my nose drips on the board. Buson is looking at the scene impersonally. The go player could be him, but it is also me, and perhaps you. He is a master at capturing such moments.

Here is another haiku that I particularly like:

mi ni shimu ya	Piercingly sad—
nakitsuma no kushi o	stepping on my dead wife's comb
neya ni fumu	in our bedroom

For whatever reason, sometime after the poet's wife has died, her comb is lying on the floor. At night, on his way to bed, he steps on something accidentally and then realizes it is her comb. A swirl of emotions shakes him: loss, grief, sorrow. This is a realistic scene from life, one that could happen to anyone.

The next poem describes the sensation of aging, under the heading "Reflection on growing old":

kyonen yori	Lonelier
mata sabishii zo	than last year—
aki no kure	the end of autumn

The older one gets, the faster the years fly by. Now another year is ending, and the poet has aged some more. Looking back over the past year, he remembers those who have died, or gone senile, or are otherwise afflicted. Life is certainly a sad thing in the end, he muses. I myself am seventy-six as I write this, and each year now I see friends die or develop Alzheimer's disease or cancer. The number keeps on growing, and there's nothing I can do about it. Such reflections are bound to make anyone feel intensely lonely. Last year was lonely too, muses the poet, but this year is lonelier still. Buson is unrivaled in his ability to evoke such feelings. His poems shrink the distance between us and bygone generations, allowing us to identify with people of times past.

Here is a poem set in summer; the heading tells us it is about "a place in

Tamba called Kaya":

natsukawa o	The joy of wading
kosu ureshisa yo	across a summer stream
te ni zōri	sandals in hand

The stream ahead is shallow. The poet slips off his sandals and wades in, reveling in the sensation of cool water on his hot, tired feet. The final phrase, "sandals in hand," brings the scene to life, and the word "joy" adds piquancy. We can well imagine the long, hot, dusty path he has been on, and his heart's leap of gratitude at the gift of coolness.

ashi yowa no	Delicate legs
watarite nigoru	wade across, muddying
haru no mizu	spring water

Here the stream is muddied, and because it is spring, the water is cold. Where a man with sturdy legs would stride briskly across, a woman with "delicate legs" gingerly slides forward, clutching her skirt to hold it above the water as her feet stir up mud. The scene is charged with sensual beauty.

Here is another haiku portraying the soft spring rain of which Buson was so fond.

harusame ya	Spring rain—
koiso no kogai	just enough to moisten
nururu hodo	small shells on the small shore

The "small shore" is undoubtedly not rugged but smooth. The rainfall is just enough so that small shells (the adjective "small" is probably unnecessary, but it matches "small shore") are faintly wet. This is a haiku of enormous charm.

Buson and the Classics

Another characteristic of Buson's haiku is that they frequently take as theme the classics, traditions, Chinese verse, and other sources that modern haiku poets influenced by realism won't touch. His haiku depicting other worlds, whether of time past or of the imagination, receive little attention or are viewed negatively, but I believe they are of definitive importance.

Anyone familiar with Chinese classics will know that Jing Ke was asked by the crown prince of Yan to assassinate Ying Zheng, the king of Qin (and eventually China's first emperor), and, after giving his solemn word to do so, set off from the banks of the Yi River. The prince saw him off in a poignant farewell with lute music. Jing Ke sang "The wind blows, the Yi River is cold. The hero leaves, never to return"—and was gone.

ekisui ni	At the Yi River—
nebuka nagaruru	leeks flowing by
samusa kana	in the cold stream

Buson's high achievement lies in his use of the image of leeks. The moment is full of tension and pathos, the scene freezing cold, but he has white leeks float past in the Yi River. There is something sublimely beautiful in his combination of this famous historical scene and the humble leek.

No one today believes in fox-possession, but Buson apparently subscribed to this once-common folk belief. Negishi Yasumori, city magistrate of Edo, wrote an essay entitled "Bag of Ears" containing many such accounts; since even a man of his education and discernment believed in foxes' power to change their shape, we can assume that the belief was widespread in Tokugawa times.

kindachi ni	A fox disguised
kitsune baketari	as a young nobleman—

yoi no haru   spring twilight

Here Buson suggests that for a fox to disguise itself as a dashing young nobleman is most fitting to the evocative hour of twilight in spring. The imaginary scene he creates is one of such beauty, it is like looking at a fine scroll painting.

Tobadono e	To Toba Palace
gorokki isogu	race five or six horsemen—
nowaki kana	autumn tempest

This is one of Buson's most famous historical poems. The horsemen are galloping through a severe storm on some unknown mission, heading to Toba Palace, the imperial villa that retired emperor Shirakawa (1053–1129) constructed near Kyoto. Along with a powerful sense of turmoil and urgency, there is a larger sense of narrative, as in a scene from an old picture scroll.

Buson wrote many such haiku, all of them compelling and dramatic. Through his historical haiku, readers come to share the culture of the Yi River, young Heian noblemen, Toba Palace, and so on. Here is one more such haiku, set in Japan's Kamakura period.

kiji naku ya	A pheasant's cry
kusa no Musashi no	in the grasses of Musashi—
hachi heiji	the eight clans

The sharp cry of the pheasant sounds in the grasses of Musashi (present-day Tokyo). Hearing it, the poet is reminded of brave men of old, the eight Taira clans of the east who rose up in Musashi to defend the capital with the resounding cry *"Iza Kamakura!"* (On to Kamakura!). This haiku too shows Buson's love of history.

AFTERWORD

The Classics Reborn

My Awakening

In closing, I would like to say something about my connection to the classics. Back in my twenties and thirties, I read nothing but European literature, chiefly works written in German. I only began reading Japanese classics at the age of forty-two. That's because in 1966, when I was forty-one, the university where I then taught gave me a year in Germany on sabbatical. In those days, when a dollar was still 360 yen and a pound 1,000 yen, few Japanese traveled to Europe. Those who scraped together a little money and made the journey waged what felt like a full-scale battle with European culture. Everybody of my generation who went to Europe in those days, including writers Kaga Otohiko[22] and Tsuji Kunio,[23] had the same harrowing experience.

Over the course of that painful year, I realized how little I knew of Japanese culture, literature, and classics—how little I knew of Japan itself. It seems strange that I should have had to go to Europe to make that sad

---

22 Kaga Otohiko (b. 1929) is a psychiatrist and author of historical fiction, including a biography of the Christian daimyo Takayama Ukon.
23 Tsuji Kunio (1925–1999), a scholar of French literature, wrote historical fiction including a life of Saigyō.

discovery, but in retrospect I can see that the outcome was inevitable. Until that point, I had immersed myself in European literature, wrapping myself in the mantle of European culture, but when I went to Europe and came face to face with the actuality of culture in that part of the world I realized to my acute discomfort that the veneer of Western culture I had acquired was totally inadequate to protect me. I was overwhelmed. Had I possessed the slightest knowledge of Japanese culture—its classics, literature, philosophy, and values—I might have been able to absorb European culture calmly while contrasting East and West. But I knew nothing. With only Western principles to go by, I felt myself disappearing within the immensity of European culture, prey to feelings of helplessness. During that year in Europe, I gradually came to feel that I had lost the identity that had sustained me until then. I came home convinced that to reestablish myself I needed to learn the culture of Japan, the land of my birth.

And so in 1967, at the age of forty-two, after returning to Japan I left off reading works in Western languages and devoted myself to Japanese classics. I bought *Gunsho ruijū*[24] and other works and read them cover to cover—all the outstanding works of Japanese classical literature. In time I developed personal preferences. The Heian period is not to my taste. I have tried more than once to read *The Tale of Genji*, without success. I am drawn to the period of transition when Kyoto-centered culture was disrupted and off to the east in Kantō—today's Tokyo area— following the Gempei War of 1180–1185, a band of warriors stepped onto history's stage by establishing the first shogunate. The monk-poet Saigyō lived then, and *Tales of the Heike* is also from that period. *Tales of Now and Long Ago*, a slightly earlier work

---

24 A collection of old books and manuscripts from ancient times through the early Tokugawa period compiled by Hanawa Hokiichi (1746–1821) with the support of the shogunate, containing 1,273 sources on topics including history, literature, religion, language, customs, art, music, education, morality, legal codes, politics, economy, society, and more. First published from 1793 to 1819. The title means "Classified Documents."

containing many stories of the difficulties encountered by people who went westward from Kantō to the Imperial Court in Kyoto, is another favorite.

One of the warriors who helped transform Japan after centuries of domination by court nobles, Shogun Minamoto no Sanetomo (1192–1219), particularly appealed to me. He was a man caught between cultures. Though he headed the rough-hewn military government in Kamakura, his sensibilities drew him to the refined culture of Kyoto, and he studied traditional *waka* poetry under the tutelage of Fujiwara no Teika. In his heart of hearts, he was loyal to the retired emperor Gotoba. His life in Kantō is portrayed in *Mirror of the East*, a detailed chronicle of the Kamakura shogunate, while his Kyoto side is portrayed in *Jottings of a Fool*, a history of Japan written around 1220 by the court priest Jien. I found it fascinating to view Sanetomo through those dual lenses, and the first book I ever wrote was a study of him.[25]

During my forties I went deeper into the world of Japanese classics. I was extremely moved to discover that traditional language and vocabulary from those earlier times survive today. I felt a kinship with the world of the classics that made me realize this was my true home. Time and again I pored over *Tales of Now and Long Ago* and *Tales of the Heike*. Neither of those works comes up in this book, but I have written elsewhere about the former.[26] Saigyō's poetry, *An Account of My Hut*, *Essays in Idleness*, *Treasury of the True Dharma Eye*, and other classics taken up in these pages also grew familiar to me as my reading expanded.

Religion entered the picture too. I developed an appreciation for the worlds of the spiritual leaders Dōgen, Hōnen and Shinran. Having never professed any religion, I always considered myself a person of no faith, but gradually I was drawn to a Buddhist way of thinking, not through modern Buddhism but through vibrant medieval writings. Then I sensed that that

25 *Sanetomo kō: Homo religiosus no bungaku* (Tokyo: Kodansha, 1972).
26 *Konjaku monogatari shū* in *Koten o yomu* Vol. 4. (Tokyo: Iwanami Shoten, 1983).

same world-view was echoed in the much later poetry of Bashō, Buson, and Ryōkan. The living continuity of Japanese tradition came home to me, and I began to feel its sustaining presence within myself.

By reading the classics I came to truly accept, validate, and believe in myself. Familiarity with the classics means not only sharing in the feelings of people of antiquity but sharing common values with our contemporaries through a shared cultural heritage. This role of culture is both vital and extraordinary.

Why Read the Classics?

After World War II, a flood tide of American culture swept over Europe and Japan. Japan's response was different from that of Europe. In its zeal to catch up with and surpass the United States, Japan wholeheartedly embraced American-style methods of production and consumption and, by enhancing the efficiency of those methods, transformed itself into an economic superpower based on mass production, mass consumption, and mass disposal. The European response is sharply contrasting. In Germany, the United Kingdom, and France, people take such fierce pride in their native culture that they automatically resist the invasion of anything that threatens it. Regarding television, for example, Germans limit their viewing to certain programs, and British parents restrict what their children are allowed to see. I have visited German and British homes and observed this with my own eyes. In this way, both societies have a built-in check mechanism against the intrusion of foreign culture.

It's the same with food. Japan has become a preeminently omnivorous nation. Not only Chinese but Italian, French, and "ethnic"—a rubric that includes the culinary traditions of various countries—cuisines are daily fare for the Japanese. Whereas before the war people ate rice for breakfast, lunch and dinner, few if any families do so now. Breakfast is likely to include some form of bread, and other meals have been transformed as well. Only Japan has experienced this kind of change. Germans follow their traditional diet to this day: for breakfast, round, hard bread and coffee; for lunch, a hot meal; and for dinner, *kaltes Essen* ("cold food"), typically a plate of bread, sausage and cheese. French people and Italians are equally adamant about sticking to traditional eating habits.

Europeans are well aware, after centuries of warfare, that only by protecting their cultural identity can they protect their country. In contrast, a cultural crisis now looms in Japan.

If classics became the shared cultural possession of a majority of Japanese, we might achieve ethnic empathy. That is why I never lose an opportunity to tout the pleasure of reading Japanese classics. But unless I speak from my own experience, from my own life principles, my words have no power to reach others.

Getting the Most Out of the Classics

Having discovered the rich treasury of Japanese classics in my forties, I realized a decade or so later that all the studying of European literature I had done in my twenties and thirties was by no means wasted. People who start by learning Japanese literature and history, or Chinese literature, inevitably apply longstanding approaches to those genres and are bound by them. They read works exactly as they were written, with the same meaning they had at that time. They spend all their time verifying facts and words, so it is extremely tough going. Those who read medieval works can speak only about the medieval period, and those who study the early modern period can speak only about that. Stuck each in their narrow slot, experts harp on trifles. This is the inevitable outcome.

In contrast, when I read a work I apply the techniques I learned in my study of Western literature. Instead of seeking the original meaning a classic may have had, I ask what meaning it has for us today. This, I truly believe, is how to get the most out of literature. What's important is not the past but living, breathing human beings now: I learned this from cultural critic Walter Benjamin (1892–1940) among others.

Following this line of thinking, what's important in reading the classics is not to grasp the entirety of a philosopher's system of thought or to read everything a given author wrote, but to fasten on one small thing a philosopher said in the course of his larger work, or one brief but key passage or turn of phrase by an author, and let it enter you and form your core, putting down roots so that it becomes an indelible part of you. This is the method I have always followed in my reading of Japanese classics.

I stated at the very beginning of this book that I deliberately examine passages of the classics out of context, that this is how I find they come to life. My approach is based on personal experience. The following comments that Goethe made in dialogue with the poet Johann Peter Eckermann express a similar idea:

> People always talk about creativity, but what does it mean? As soon as we are born, the world begins to influence us, and continues doing so until we die. Do we have anything of our own apart from our energy, strength, and will? If I could list everything I owe to my great precursors and contemporaries, very little would be left.[27]

I was astonished to think that the creative genius Goethe would say such a thing, but as I have grown older I have come to think that he was by no

---

27 Kameo Eishirō, trans. *Gēte to no taiwa*, Vol. 1 (Tokyo: Iwanami Bunko, 1949).

means being humble but very likely expressing his true feeling. We create ourselves by reading works left behind by our many great predecessors; such creativity as we have lies in our manner of creating ourselves, he implies, a process that takes place via our ancient cultural heritage.

Reading Goethe, I came to think of myself as one knot in the vast net of culture, and so I am. As he says, however many books we read, it's only a small part of the whole. If we read Bashō, that's not enough. Only when certain words by Bashō or Buson or Dōgen enter us and put down roots in our hearts do they come alive and grow.

Let me give a couple of examples. "If we hate death, we should love life. Let us take pleasure in the joy of living day by day." This quotation from Section 93 of *Essays in Idleness* by Yoshida Kenkō, with its call to savor afresh every day the joy of being alive, has entered deep within me, taken root and given rise to many new thoughts. "In the revelation of the immeasurable Dharma within the self there is life, and there is death." This line from *Treasury of the True Dharma Eye* has also stayed with me. The Dharma is that which maintains and sustains. Culture, when it becomes part of you, is a sustaining power. Filled with the Dharma, one holds both life and death; the Dharma is universal life. Statements like these I commit to memory by reading them over and over again. Then when the occasion arises, they emerge from my mouth and sustain me.

Gradually, as such things take possession of us and we are indeed possessed by culture, we come to identify with it. Dōgen also wrote, "By the spiritual discipline I undergo I acquire the Dharma, so I ought to love and honor myself." Feelings of self-love and self-respect come not because I am great but because within me I contain the Dharma (for which read "truth" or "culture"). Anyone who cannot respect himself cannot respect others either; such respect is the byproduct of shared values, shared Dharma or heritage.

When I encounter words that speak to me, even short scraps, I make a note of them. I call the resulting collection my "black book" and have kept it for a long time, to this very day. Now and then I look through what I have written and realize that the words have contributed to making me who I am. Stendhal, for example, wrote in *On Love*, "I fear nothing but what I respect." That is definitely the basis for a certain philosophy or way of thinking; I sense in the words a system of thought that continues to affect me. Sometimes it is a single poem that often comes to mind, like this one by Saigyō: "On Mt. Yoshino/ snowflakes scatter/on cherry branches—/this is one of those years/when the blossoms will be late." I feel the words working on my sensibilities, nourishing my spirit. When I murmur Buson's haiku "Banked fire—/my hermitage likewise/buried in the snow" or "With Bashō gone/the year still cannot/ come to an end," the latter written after the master's death when there was no one to take his place in the world of *haikai*, the words nurture my aesthetic sense and shape my approach to, or stance regarding, the literary arts.

"At last, having no ability or skill, I followed this one course": this line from Bashō's *Knapsack Notebook* reminds me that even the great poet applied the words "no ability" to himself. At the same time, I can see that he took pride in having followed a single course throughout his life. It gives me courage.

Shaping the Self

In this way, applying the classics to modern times does not consist in nostalgic longing for the past but rather in perceiving the thoughts and feelings of the ancients in the words they left us and discovering therein the strength to live in our modern world. Their words also provide nourishment for us to grow.

I am keenly aware that by applying the classics to modern life, I have been able to use their strength to shape myself. It is the classics that have made me who I am today. They do not live within me intact in their original form; rather, I remake them and thereby create fresh cells in myself. This is what it means to breathe life into the classics and for the classics to breathe life into me. Gradually I have come to see that this two-way process is at the heart of living culture.

In that sense, the failure of today's young people to read books is truly a critical situation. Ideology, systems of thought, are based on words. Without words, systematic thought and communication, as well as self-cultivation, are impossible. Words are not everything, but without them, we cannot become our true selves. The words of the classics are especially vital. Years ago when I was a student, an elderly teacher of mine used to say time and again, "Don't read new books till they have been out three years. Read the classics." I was young, and I ignored his advice, thinking, "What does he know?" Age has taught me that he was right.

We do not become human simply by being born or by being alive. The state of society today makes this eminently plain. Every other species of animal cares for its young; the inability of some people to do so means that too many of us are not human. Juvenile crime is a social issue, and every time an incident occurs I wonder to what extent the offender has developed as a human being. Too many people never go through the necessary discipline.

It is by learning, and mastering what we have learned, that we become human. Too many of today's politicians strike me as lacking the ability to distinguish between right and wrong. They are ruining Japan. We must recreate a climate in which people value the cultural heritage of our ancestors, appreciate how interesting and valuable it is, and use it as nourishment to develop ourselves. This is how to nurture appreciation of beauty, a sense of right and wrong, and the ability to tell what is grotesque. Then we can at last share our cultural heritage and become human beings shaped by it. Dōgen wrote, "To have a mind and body suitable for ceaseless practice you must love and honor yourself." Only by doing these things, I believe, can we gain the ability to love and honor ourselves.

A Guide to Titles Cited in the Text

An Account of My Hut	*Hōjōki*
Analects	*Lunyu*
"Bag of Ears"	*Mimibukuro*
"The Beautiful View from the Cemetery"	*Utsukushii bochi kara no nagame*
The Book of Life-Nourishing Principles	*Yōjōkun*
Classified Documents	*Gunsho ruijū*
Collection of Gathered Gems	*Shūgyokushū*
Collection of Religious Awakenings	*Hosshinshū*
Collection of Ten Thousand Leaves	*Man'yōshū*
Conversations with Saigyō	*Saikōdanshō*
Curious Accounts of the Zen Monk Ryōkan	*Ryōkan zenshi kiwa*
Essays in Idleness	*Tsurezuregusa*
From the Abyss of Death	*Shi no fuchi yori*
Guidelines for Studying the Way	*Gakudōyō yōjinshū*
Heart Sutra	*Hannya shingyō*
History of the Tōdaiji Great Buddha Hall	*Tōdaiji daibutsuden engi*
Jottings of a Fool	*Gukanshō*
Knapsack Notebook	*Oi no kobumi*
Mirror of the East	*Azuma kagami*
Mountain Home Collection	*Sankashū*
Nameless Notes	*Mumyōshō*
New Collection of Waka Ancient and Modern	*Shinkokin wakashū*
Notes of a Frog at the Bottom of a Well	*Seiashō*
On Impermanence	*Mujō to iu koto*

On Love	De l'amour
"One-sheet Document"	Ichimai kishōmon
A Prologue to "Medicine for Dying"	"Shi no igaku" e no joshō
The Rustic Gate	Saimon no ji
Saga Diary	Saga nikki
Secret Teachings of the Retired Emperor Gotoba	Gotobain gokuden
Supplement to Things Heard and Noted	Zanshū
The Tale of Genji	Genji monogatari
Tales of the Heike	Heike monogatari
Tales of Now and Long Ago	Konjaku monogatari
Tales of Saigyō	Saigyō monogatari
Things Heard and Noted	Kikigakishū
Treasury of the True Dharma Eye	Shōbōgenzō
"Actualizing the Absolute"	Genjō kōan
"Ancient Mirror"	Kokyō
"Ceaseless Practice"	Gyōji
"Life and Death"	Shōji
"Mountains and Water Sutra"	Sansuikyō
"On Functioning Fully"	Zenki
"On Learning the Way through Body and Mind"	Shinjin gakudō
"The One Bright Pearl"	Ikka myōju
"Time-Being"	Uji
Treasury of the True Dharma Eye: Record of Things Heard	Shōbōgenzō zuimonki
The Way and Its Power	Tao te ching
Universal Recommendation for Zazen	Fukan zazengi
Words of Warning	Kaigo

References

Ryōkan

Ejō, ed. *Shōbōgenzō zuimonki*. Revised by Watsuji Tetsurō. Iwanami Bunko, Iwanami Shoten, 1982.

Karaki Junzō. *Ryōkan* in *Nihon shijinsen*, vol. 20. Chikuma Shobo, 1971.

Matsumoto Ichiju. *Ryōkan*. Haruki Bunko, Kadokawa Haruki Jimusho, 2000.

Nihon Keizai Shimbunsha, ed. *Ryōkan-san* (catalog of an exhibition commemorating the 170th anniversary of his death). Nihon Keizai Shimbunsha, 2000.

Nishigōri Kyūgo, ed. *Hokuetsu ijin shamon Ryōkan zenden*. Shozansha, 1980.

Ōhashi Shunnō, ed. *Hōnen, Ippen* in *Nihon shisō taikei*, vol. 10. Iwanami Shoten, 1971.

Ōshima Kasoku and Harada Kampei, eds. *Yakuchū Ryōkan shishū*. Iwanami Bunko, Iwanami Shoten, 1941.

Tanikawa Toshirō. *Ryōkan no shōgai to itsuwa*. Kobunsha, 1984.

Yoshino Hideo. *Ryōkan*. Art Deizu, 2001.

Yoshino Hideo, ed. *Ryōkan kashū*. Tōyō Bunko, Heibonsha, 1992.

Yoshida Kenkō

Aries, Philippe. *Shi to rekishi. (Essais sur l'histoire de la mort en occident du moyen age a nos jours)* Translated by Itō Akira and Naruse Komao. Misuzu Shobo, 1983.

Nishio Minoru and Yasuraoka Kōsaku, eds. *Shintei Tsurezuregusa*. Iwanami Bunko, Iwanami Shoten, 1985.

Ōoka Shōhei. *Ōoka Shōhei zenshū*, vol. 2. Chikuma Shobo, 1994.

Ozaki Kazuo. *Utsukushii bochi kara no nagame*. Kodansha Bungei Bunko, Kodansha, 1998.

Takami Jun. *Shi no fuchi yori*. Kodansha Bungei Bunko, Kodansha, 1993.

Yanagida Kunio. *"Shi no igaku" e no joshō*. Shincho Bunko, Shinchosha, 1990.

Kamo no Chōmei

Ichiko Teiji, ed. *Shintei Hōjōki.* Iwanami Bunko, Iwanami Shoten, 1989.

Minamoto no Ienaga Nikki Kenkyūkai. *Minamoto no Ienaga nikki: Kōhon, kenkyū, sōsakuin.* Kazama Shobo, 1985.

Satake Akihiro and Kubota Jun, eds. *Hōjōki Tsurezuregusa* in *Shin Nihon koten bungaku taikei,* vol. 39. Iwanami Shoten, 1989.

Yanase Kazuo, ed. *Kōchū Kamo no Chōmei zenshū.* Kazama Shobo, 1989.

Dōgen

Dōgen. *Shōbōgenzō,* vol. 1. Edited and annotated by Mizuno Yaoko. Iwanami Bunko, Iwanami Shoten, 1990.

Dōgen. *Shōbōgenzō,* vol. 2. Edited and annotated by Mizuno Yaoko. Iwanami Bunko, Iwanami Shoten, 1990.

Dōgen. *Shōbōgenzō,* vol. 3. Edited and annotated by Mizuno Yaoko. Iwanami Bunko, Iwanami Shoten, 1991.

Dōgen. *Shōbōgenzō,* vol. 4. Edited and annotated by Mizuno Yaoko. Iwanami Bunko, Iwanami Shoten, 1993.

Suzuki Daisetsu. *Shimpen Tōyōteki na mikata.* Edited by Ueda Shizuteru. Iwanami Bunko, Iwanami Shoten, 1997.

Ueda Shizuteru. *Meister Eckhart* in *Jinrui no chiteki isan,* vol. 21. Kodansha, 1998.

Saigyō

Hanawa Hokiichi, ed. *Gunsho ruijū,* vol. 16. Zoku Gunshoruiju Kanseikai, 1934.

Hanawa Hokiichi, ed. *Zoku Gunsho ruijū,* vol. 16. Supplemented by Ōta Tōshirō. Zoku Gunshoruijū Kanseikai, 1925.

Hisamatsu Sen'ichi and Nishio Minoru, eds. *Karonshū, Nōgakuronshū* in *Nihon koten bungaku taikei,* vol. 65. Iwanami Shoten, 1961.

Kajihara Masaaki and Yamashita Hiroaki, eds. *Heike monogatari* (2). Iwanami Bunko, Iwanami Shoten, 1999.

Kobayashi Hideo. *Mozart, Mujō to iu koto.* Shincho Bunko, Shinchosha, 1991.

Kubota Jun and Yamaguchi Akiho, eds. *Myōe shōnin shū.* Iwanami Bunko, Iwanami Shoten, 1981.

Nakamura Shunjō, ed. *Bashō kikō bunshū.* Iwanami Bunko, Iwanami Shoten, 1971.

Ryō Susumu, ed. *Azuma kagami* (2). Iwanami Bunko, Iwanami Shoten, 1940.

Sasaki Nobutsuna, ed. *Shintei Sankashū.* Iwanami Bunko, Iwanami Shoten, 1939.

Sugiura Shōichirō, Miyamoto Saburō, and Ogino Kiyoshi, eds. *Bashō bunshū* in *Nihon koten bungaku taikei,* vol. 46. Iwanami Shoten, 1959.

Taga Munehaya, ed. *Kōhon Shūgyokushū.* Yoshikawa Kobunkan, 1971.

Ueda Miyoji. *Kono yo kono sei.* Shinchosha, 1984.

Yasuda Akio. *Saigyō.* Yayoi Sensho, Yayoi Shobo, 1973.

Yosa Buson

Asahi Shimbunsha, ed. *Buson sono futatsu no tabi* (exhibition catalog). Asahi Shimbunsha, 2001.

Hagiwara Sakutarō. *Kyōshū no shijin Yosa Buson.* Iwanami Bunko, Iwanami Shoten, 1988.

Ogata Tsutomu, ed. *Buson haikushū.* Iwanami Bunko, Iwanami Shoten, 1989.

Yajima Nagisao. *Yosa Buson sansaku.* Kadokawa Shoten, 1995.

The Classics Reborn

Eckermann, Johann Peter. *Goethe to no taiwa*, vol. 1. Translated by Kameo Eishirō. Iwanami Bunko, Iwanami Shoten, 1940.

Nakano Kōji, *Koten o yomu: Konjaku monogatari shū*. Iwanami Dōjidai Library, Iwanami Shoten, 1996.

Nakano Kōji, *Sanetomo kō*. Kodansha Bungei Bunko, Kodansha, 2000.

THE AUTHOR GRATEFULLY ACKNOWLEDGES THE ASSISTANCE OF THE FOLLOWING:

Ryōkan Memorial Museum

Kanagawa Prefectural Kanazawa-Bunko Museum

Hayashibara Museum of Art

Head Temple Eiheiji

Manno Art Museum

Itsuō Art Museum

Mutō Haruta

Nakano Kōji (1925–2004)

Born in Ichikawa, Chiba Prefecture, he studied on his own and entered the prestigious Fifth High School in Kumamoto. After a stint in the armed forces during the Pacific War, he graduated from the German Literature Department of the University of Tokyo. Starting in 1952, he taught for twenty-eight years at Kokugakuin University while translating the works of modern writers such as Franz Kafka, Erich Nossack, and Günter Grass. In 1966, he went to Europe for a year as a research scholar. On his return, he immersed himself in Japanese medieval literature and began writing literary criticism, novels, and essays. His first book, a study of Shogun Minamoto no Sanetomo, came out in 1972. His book *Bruegel e no tabi* (Journey to Bruegel), inspired by his encounters overseas with Western paintings, validates the first half of his life while creating a distinctive worldview. He wrote various award-winning books including the autobiographical novel *Mugi ururu hi ni* (When the Wheat Ripens); *Harasu no ita hibi* (Days with Haras), a memoir of his departed dog; and *Seihin no shisō* (The Concept of Honest Poverty). From 1993 he served as director of the Kanagawa Literature Association. His final book was *Seneca: Gendaijin e no tegami* (Seneca: Letters to People of Today). Throughout his prolific writing career, Nakano explored the nature of true happiness, offering words of warning and encouragement for modern Japanese.

Juliet Winters Carpenter (b. 1948)

A prolific translator of Japanese literature, she was born in Ann Arbor, Michigan, and grew up in Evanston, Illinois. Her lifelong interest in Japan was triggered by a 1960 visit with her father. Her first translated book, *Secret Rendezvous* (*Mikkai*), by Abe Kōbō, received the 1980 Japan-US Friendship Commission Prize for the Translation of Japanese Literature. *A True Novel*, her translation of Minae Mizumura's *Honkaku shōsetsu*, received the same award in 2014. Current projects include Shiba Ryōtarō's *Ryōma ga yuku* and Mizumura's *Shishōsetsu from left to right*. She has lived in Japan continuously since 1975 and teaches English at Doshisha Women's College of Liberal Arts in Kyoto.

（英文版）いまを生きる知恵

WORDS TO LIVE BY: Japanese Classics for Our Time

2018年3月27日　第1刷発行

著　　者　　中野 孝次
訳　　者　　ジュリエット・カーペンター
発 行 所　　一般財団法人 出版文化産業振興財団
　　　　　　〒101-0051 東京都千代田区神田神保町3-12-3
　　　　　　電話　03-5211-7282（代）
ホームページ　http://www.jpic.or.jp/

印刷・製本所　大日本印刷株式会社